Participatory Journalism in Africa

T0373532

This book offers an African perspective on how news organisations are embracing digital participatory practices as part of their everyday news production, dissemination and audience engagement strategies.

Drawing on empirical evidence from news organisations in sub-Saharan Africa, *Participatory Journalism in Africa* investigates and maps out professional practices emerging with journalists' direct interactions with readers and sources via online user comment spaces and social media platforms. Using a social constructivist approach, the book focuses on the challenges relating to the elite-centric nature of active participation on the platforms, while also highlighting emerging ethical and normative dilemmas. The authors also point to the hidden structural controls to participation and user engagement associated with artificial intelligence, chatbots and algorithms. These obstacles, coupled with low digital literacy levels and the well-established pitfalls of the digital divide, challenge the utopian view that in Africa interactive digital technologies are the *sine qua non* spaces for democratic participation.

This is a valuable resource for academics, journalists and students across a wide range of disciplines including journalism studies, communication, sociology and political science.

Hayes Mawindi Mabweazara (PhD) teaches media and international journalism at the University of Glasgow, UK, where he is a member of the Glasgow University Media Group. He is Associate Editor of *Journalism Studies* and *African Journalism Studies*, and a Research Associate at the University of Johannesburg's Faculty of Humanities. His most recent publication is the edited volume *Newsmaking Cultures in Africa* (2018).

Admire Mare (PhD) is an Associate Professor and Deputy Head in the Department of Communication at the Namibia University of Science and Technology, Windhoek, Namibia. He is a Research Associate at the University of Johannesburg's Faculty of Humanities. He currently leads the international research project *Social Media, Misinformation and Elections in Kenya and Zimbabwe* (SoMeKeZi) funded by the Social Science Research Council (2019–2021).

Disruptions: Studies in Digital Journalism
Series editor: Bob Franklin

Disruptions refers to the radical changes provoked by the affordances of digital technologies that occur at a pace and on a scale that disrupts settled understandings and traditional ways of creating value, interacting and communicating both socially and professionally. The consequences for digital journalism involve far reaching changes to business models, professional practices, roles, ethics, products and even challenges to the accepted definitions and understandings of journalism. For Digital Journalism Studies, the field of academic inquiry which explores and examines digital journalism, disruption results in paradigmatic and tectonic shifts in scholarly concerns. It prompts reconsideration of research methods, theoretical analyses and responses (oppositional and consensual) to such changes, which have been described as being akin to 'a moment of mind-blowing uncertainty'.

Routledge's new book series, *Disruptions: Studies in Digital Journalism*, seeks to capture, examine and analyse these moments of exciting and explosive professional and scholarly innovation which characterize developments in the day-to-day practice of journalism in an age of digital media, and which are articulated in the newly emerging academic discipline of Digital Journalism Studies.

Participatory Journalism in Africa
Digital News Engagement and User Agency in the South
Hayes Mawindi Mabweazara and Admire Mare

Disrupting Investigative Journalism
Amanda Gearing

Journalism Education for the Digital Age
Promises, Perils, and Possibilities
Brian Creech

For more information, please visit: www.routledge.com/Disruptions/book-series/DISRUPTDIGJOUR

Participatory Journalism in Africa

Digital News Engagement and User Agency in the South

Hayes Mawindi Mabweazara and Admire Mare

LONDON AND NEW YORK

First published 2021
by Routledge
2 Park Square, Milton Park, Abingdon, Oxon OX14 4RN

and by Routledge
605 Third Avenue, New York, NY 10158

Routledge is an imprint of the Taylor & Francis Group, an informa business

© 2021 Hayes Mawindi Mabweazara and Admire Mare

British Library Cataloguing-in-Publication Data
A catalogue record for this book is available from the British Library

Library of Congress Cataloging-in-Publication Data
Names: Mabweazara, Hayes Mawindi, 1977- author. |
Mare, Admire, author.
Title: Participatory journalism in Africa : digital news engagement and user agency in the south / Hayes Mawindi Mabweazara and Admire Mare.
Description: New York : Routledge, 2021. |
Series: Disruptions: studies in digital journalism |
Includes bibliographical references and index. |
Identifiers: LCCN 2020053779 | ISBN 9780367197292 (hardback) |
ISBN 9780429242908 (ebook)
Subjects: LCSH: Online journalism--Africa, Sub-Saharan. |
Journalism--Technological innovations--Africa, Sub-Saharan. |
Citizen journalism--Africa, Sub-Saharan.
Classification: LCC PN4784.O62 M33 2021 | DDC 076--dc23
LC record available at https://lccn.loc.gov/2020053779

ISBN: 978-0-367-19729-2 (hbk)
ISBN: 978-1-032-00213-2 (pbk)
ISBN: 978-0-429-24290-8 (ebk)

Typeset in Times New Roman
by Taylor & Francis Books

Hayes Mawindi Mabweazara:
For my partner, Chengetai

Admire Mare:
For Evelyn (Grace Chipo) and Akudzweishe (Kuku)

Contents

Figures

Acknowledgements

Although we have only a very limited space here to make acknowledgements for assistance, there are several people who have contributed to the realisation of this book in countless ways, large and small – we are deeply thankful. It is difficult to see how this book would ever have materialised without the astounding generosity and patience of the Disruptions book series editor, Professor Bob Franklin. Beyond extending the invitation to contribute to the series and his belief in our suitability to write the book, we are permanently indebted and thankful for the endless deadline extensions, constant prodding and dogged determination to see the project come to fruition. Bob's strong conviction in the need to balance scholarly accounts, geopolitical contexts and voices in efforts to understand the multiple complexities of contemporary 'disruptions' in journalism – a major impetus behind the writing of this book – is without doubt one of his major contributions to a field he has worked exceptionally hard to develop and champion.

It is undeniable that a project of this nature inevitably benefits from the support of those most directly affected by the time and attention it demands to complete. Much of this book was written at the outset of the Covid-19 pandemic and during the excruciatingly difficult lockdown period. Hayes would like to express his heartfelt thanks to his wife, Chengetai and sons, Tanaka and Nyasha for their deep sacrifices, enduring support, patience and encouragement throughout the writing of the book. Their names may not be on the cover of the book, but they gave so much that this work is equally their own. Thanks are also due to colleagues within the Glasgow University Media Group and the Digital Societies Research Group, who have equally been a source of inspiration and invaluable insights, albeit unbeknown to them – Catherine Happer, Greg Philo, Alison Eldridge, Catriona Forrest, Bridgett Wessels, Andy Hoskins, Justine Gangneux, and many others. The conversations we have had across seminars, meetings and in the corridors of Adam Smith

Building during 'normal' times are silently weaved into some of the chapters and sections of this book. Matt Dawson, Head of Sociology at the University of Glasgow has been exceptionally supportive in many ways than can be summed up here. Thank you for fostering an invigorating and collegial working environment.

Admire would like to dedicate this book to his wife, Evelyn (Grace Chipo) and son Akudzweishe (Kuku) for allowing him to spend countless hours away from the comfort of their presence as he worked on the manuscript. Their unwavering support and encouragement enabled him to soldier on despite the many challenges and competing deadlines he had to contend with. He also thanks his parents (Reuben and Daisy) and siblings, whose support he will always cherish. Heartfelt thanks are also extended to colleagues at the University of Johannesburg's Department of Journalism, Film and Television and Namibia University of Science and Technology's Department of Communication. Besides promoting working environments conducive to productivity, colleagues at the two universities have been instrumental in supporting Admire's research agenda, both morally and financially. He particularly thanks Jane Duncan and Herman Wasserman for believing in him even when he doubted himself while pursuing his PhD studies.

Questions on who has contributed what in a co-authored book are sometimes inevitable. This project is, in many ways, testimony to the scholarly synergies we have developed over the last couple of years and writing it together has been a deeply fulfilling experience. We are privileged to work in closely related research areas, and to have collaborated in a couple of projects before co-authoring this book. In writing the book, we worked collaboratively and creatively across *every* chapter – reviewing, critiquing and rewriting – in ways that benefitted immensely from a close familiarity with each other's work. We are therefore collectively responsible for the arguments contained in each and every chapter of the book.

Acronyms and abbreviations

AI	Artificial intelligence
AMH	Alpha Media Holdings (Zimbabwe)
ANC	African National Congress
BBC	British Broadcasting Corporation
BVR	Biometric Voter Registration, Zimbabwe
CGTN	China Global Television Network
CMS	Content management systems
CNN	Cable News Network
DL	Deep learning
4IR	Fourth Industrial Revolution
FAQs	Frequently Asked Questions
H-to-H	Human to human interactions
H-to-nH	Human and non-human interactions
ML	Machine learning
MDC-T	Movement for Democratic Change – Tsvangirai
NBC	Namibia Broadcasting Corporation
SMS	Short message service
SABC	South African Broadcasting Corporation
UGC	User generated content
WAN-IFRA	World Association of Newspapers and News Publishers
ZANU-PF	Zimbabwe African National Union – Patriotic Front
ZBC	Zimbabwe Broadcasting Corporation
ZEC	Zimbabwe Electoral Commission
Zimpapers	Zimbabwe Newspapers group

1 The participatory turn in African journalism

Context and conceptualisations

Despite the fact that Africa is the least connected continent on the Internet and its associated digital technologies (Nyamnjoh 2005; Mabweazara 2017), traditional journalism has not escaped the complexities and contradictions associated with the 1990s crusade towards the adoption of digital technologies in journalism. There is a consensus among scholars that journalists on the continent, like their counterparts in the rest of the world, are experiencing the disruptive impact of these digital technologies on the way they gather, produce and distribute news (Paterson 2013; Mabweazara et al., 2014; Mare 2014). Audiences, which until recent years were imaginary figures in the minds of journalists (Singer et al., 2011) – hidden behind live radio phone-in commentaries or letters to the editor – now clearly manifest themselves online in various forms, including commenting directly on stories, writing on blogs attached to news websites, WhatsApping, Tweeting or Facebooking in ways that challenge and complement journalists' traditional roles as sole arbiters and purveyors of information. As elsewhere, the manifestation of audiences in online platforms have given rise to editorial metrics and analytic tools which are enabling newsrooms to monitor and evaluate granular details about audiences' news consumption and engagement practices (see Moyo D. et al., 2019). Readers' online comments in particular are proving to be a popular route for participatory journalism, giving readers 'agency [and] authority to influence news making' (Hermida 2011a, 14). Platforms which enable readers to comment, share and deliberate on stories have become near ubiquitous in even the poorest regions of Africa where they are accessed mainly via smartphones, thus providing one of the most pragmatic and influential attributes and functionality of the digital era.

Serious structural changes are underway – content is undergoing radical changes; old operational and business models have been *disrupted*. Similarly, news consumptions habits and practices are finding new definitions on the web as audiences look for as well as share news content 'in iterative consumption practices that challenge as well as complement traditional news flows' (Mabweazara 2015a, 11). News organisations on the African continent are clearly undergoing an unprecedented state of turmoil, as developments that previously seemed distant have gradually become an inescapable reality, reinforcing but largely threatening established professional ideals as well as the social function of journalism. Responses to these disruptive tendencies have not been uniform as some media organisations have opted to open the floodgates of participatory journalism while others have erected impenetrable walls.

While a rich corpus of research on digital participatory practices and cultures is emerging, mainly from Western scholarship (see for example, Singer et al. 2011; Batsell 2015; Lewis 2015; Barney et al. 2016), in Africa such research is scarce. To date, there are no studies focusing primarily on *participatory journalism* in Africa both as a concept and social practice – it's daily practices and characteristics, including how journalists are thinking about and dealing with it – even as it has become apparent that the Internet and its associated digital technologies are no longer just basic tools for the practice of journalism in African newsrooms (Mabweazara 2015a; Mare 2014). What remains particularly uncertain is how mainstream news organisations and their journalists are adapting to new audience participatory platforms, how they are forging 'new' ways of engaging with their readers and sources and, more importantly, how they have adjusted their professional notions in terms of which traditions have survived and which have needed rethinking. This is particularly important in the context of a number of setbacks related to the 'digital divide', including the complexities and contradictions associated with the disproportionate diffusion and permeation of new digital technologies into African journalism practice.

The paucity of studies that empirically discriminate between what could or should be universal professional practices and what might be context-dependent practices of participatory journalism in Africa (Mabweazara et al. 2014) has meant that norms and practices emerging from Western scholarship are often 'applied out of context, sometimes awkwardly' (Ibelema 2008, 36). Indeed, the performance of journalism in Africa is all too often measured against the backdrop of Western standards. While theories and empirical studies developed in the West might appear to be applicable in Africa, closer consideration reveals that adapting these studies is not always straightforward since they cover only a small portion of developments and experiences in Africa, which are often less clear-cut and resistant to any attempts to simplify them (Nyamnjoh 1999). Local socio-political and economic factors that shape and underlie practices are often overlooked. However, as Nyamnjoh (1999, 15) rightly avers, African journalism research must be located 'in African realities and not in Western fantasies'. This is particularly important for the production of context-specific studies, which are grounded in local experiences and world views.

Against this background, this book is an initial effort at exploring the intricacies of *participatory journalism* in sub-Saharan Africa – it specifically explores how current developments in audience participation are redefining journalistic cultures, values and practices. By focusing on a range of African countries, we do not take for granted the important differences between African countries nor do we attempt to flatten and legitimate inequalities between them by assuming any semblance of homogeneity in the countries themselves. The plurality of the conditions in which African journalists operate has been highlighted by a number of researchers who challenge the popular misconception of treating Africa 'as a country rather than as a diverse continent which comprises of a large number of countries and is host to a wide variety of [cultures, languages and economies]' (Willems & Mano 2016, 5). These critics foreground the fact that the continent is diverse and complex, and so is the rate at which digital technologies, including the Internet, are adopted in newsmaking contexts. Obonyo (2011, 5) reminds us that 'Africa does not provide a clear picture that is easy to diagnose'. The enormity and complexity of Africa makes it difficult to paint the continent's 'digital' journalistic cultures with a single brush (Mabweazara 2015a). Consequently, while broadly foregrounding the general structural differences between the Global North and the South, in this book we attempt to transcend these boundaries by acknowledging the fact that *there is not just one but multiple digital cultures*. Thus, while situating participatory journalism in the lived experiences of the South, sub-Saharan Africa in this case, we equally confront the homogenising nature of the North/South divide by advancing the fact that these regions are not homogenous landscapes with collective singular identities. Rather, they have important complexities and nuances with and between them.

Our interest therefore is in offering an alternative understanding of *participatory journalism* outside the dominant body of knowledge emerging from Western scholarship, especially Europe and America, which continues to frame the debates by means of Western concerns, contexts, user-behaviour-patterns and theories, thus creating a kind of 'digital universalism' that glosses over *differences* and *cultural specificities*. Thus, this book foregrounds the importance of appreciating some kind of 'digital particularism' associated with participatory journalism in Africa. We highlight that there are other 'knowledges' or 'epistemologies' of digital journalism, which can help us to understand the plurality and complexities of 'digital disruptions' to journalism that exist in the 21st century. Thus, Western-centric conceptions cannot be taken as the sole point of departure when unpacking or conceptualising digital participatory experiences across the globe (Willems & Mano 2016). Equally, countries of the South cannot always be framed as inherently 'different', 'alternative' or lagging behind. As Nyamnjoh aptly explains, in 'contexts where ordinary people are peripheral to global trends and subjected to the high-handedness and repression of their own governments' as is the case in most sub-Saharan African countries, 'it is easy to slip into metanarratives that celebrate victimhood' (2005, 204).

The book, therefore, contributes to conversations that confront the entrenched universalism in journalism and media studies by engaging in a dialogue with traditions, epistemologies and experiences in ways that foreground the plurality, diversity and cultural richness of digital experiences across a range of contexts (Mabweazara 2015a). As Willems and Mano (2016, 9) contend, 'it is essential to conduct audience (and user) research from multiple vantage points [...] to produce pluriversal accounts of audiences and users globally which may or may not challenge the often-assumed universality of existing research'. In many ways, user behaviours are shaped by socio-political and economic circumstances, hence the need to guard against blindly universalising participatory journalism experiences.

Towards a conceptual understanding of 'participatory journalism'

The term *participatory journalism* has in recent years been deployed as a self-explanatory social practice associated with new audience *participatory practices* facilitated by new interactive digital technologies. While this is largely true, the notion of *audience participation*, however, has a long history that predates the digital age (Barney et al. 2016). In other words, journalism has always been participatory and interactive in more ways than can possibly be covered in this book. Consider, for example, radio phone-ins and letters to the editor. In the era of digital media, as with the period before, it has not always been particularly clear or obvious when that 'participation' translates into *journalism* (this book partly seeks to address this conceptual dilemma from an African perspective). The conceptual dilemma is further complicated by an abundance of closely related terms that are often used interchangeably or in place of *participatory journalism* such as *audience-driven journalism; networked journalism; collaborative journalism; conversational journalism; dialogical journalism; interactive journalism; citizen journalism* etc.

Participatory journalism, both as a concept and social practice, is therefore a generally slippery term – it needs to be problematised and placed into context. This undertaking inevitably invokes questions around the *ontology* of journalism – its very *nature* and *form*. It strikes right to the very heart of the existential question: 'what constitutes journalism in the era of disruptive interactive digital technologies?' The main challenge, in attempting to find answers to this question, as Ryfe explains, arises from the fact that 'there has never been a time in which more news is produced than today', and yet so little of it is 'produced by journalists' (2019, 206). He adds that 'journalists find themselves standing cheek by jowl with a vast array of other news producers' (Ryfe 2019, 206) in the field they once monopolised. Many of these are ordinary citizens who have never been anywhere near a journalism training school or a newsroom, yet 'they produce and distribute as much if not more news as journalists' (Ryfe 2019, 206). Where they do not produce content of their own, they take advantage of the ever-growing interactive features of digital technologies to leave their mark on the Web by *uploading images/videos*, *liking* and *sharing* content as well as *commenting* on news stories (Olsson & Svensson 2012; Suau & Pere 2014) – expressing real 'textured information about their experience of different media' (Markham 2017, 169). Rapid advancements in technology have also resulted in new approaches to generating news, including the development of automated journalism which involves the strategic deployment of artificial intelligence, chatbots and algorithms by newsrooms. This automation of news or interaction between human and non-human actors is slowly reconfiguring journalism and presenting unprecedented challenges on the normative identity of news.

Under these developments, as Ryfe contends, the question of '*what journalism is, and is for, and how it is to be distinguished from an array of other*' content, including news and associated automated practices (Ryfe 2019, 206, emphasis added), re-emerges with renewed impetus. It is a question we cannot escape across all corners of the globe but one that traditional journalists themselves dare not to confront or find the right answers to. As a result, we are confronted with a diversity of voices on what exactly constitutes *participatory journalism*. Some journalists and their news organisations are clearly uneasy with the weakening of their power as 'all-knowing' purveyors of 'truth' (Singer et al. 2011; Mabweazara 2017). Equally, the pervasive lack of clearly thought out coherent approaches or policies relating to audience participation and engagement as well as how to deal with the influx of user generated content (UGC) across news organisations, especially in the Global South, is telling.

In addressing the foregoing definitional and conceptual dilemmas of *participatory journalism*, in this book we deliberately avoid the strictures of a rigid definition given the ever-evolving nature of digital technologies, and opt for a flexible conceptualisation anchored in three intricately connected variants associated with participatory journalism as a practice in Africa:

1   Practices rooted in the *generic technological affordances* of interactive digital technologies which constitute 'invited' and most obvious 'spaces' of audience participation and can be seen as banal and universal in their visibility and popularity.
2   *Automated participatory practices*, which are rooted in the intersection between human and non-human actors and are seen as sophisticated but deeply insidious forms of participation in which ordinary citizens respond to and engage with automated cues, albeit unaware of the hidden structural manipulations 'behind the scenes'.
3   Finally, we consider *context-specific participatory practices and cultures*, in which ordinary citizens wield more agency in inventing, driving as well as shaping the interactive and participatory practices.

These three broad variants collectively constitute the complex ecology of *participatory journalism* in Africa as summed up in Figure 1.1. In our view, this conceptualisation captures the multiple, complex and sometimes contradictory elements of participatory journalism across African countries, and most importantly, it submits to the fact that in the light of 'the proliferation of non-traditional models of journalism, from online journalism outlets and mobile platforms to microblogs and social media', there 'is of course no monolithic journalism' (Usher 2016, 4). The third variant is particularly important as it highlights how *context* shapes notions of participation beyond the predetermined structures of digital technologies. It directs us to 'think beyond accounts that […] simply equate [participatory journalism] to the rise of digital technologies' (Barney et al. 2016, xi). It goes without saying that technologies are, by their nature, intimately bound up with 'multiple domains of social, political, economic and cultural practice' (Barney et al. 2016, xi). Thus, although they are imbued with inbuilt ('preferred') participatory affordances, in this book we broadly argue that it is the situated users who negotiate and creatively appropriate them resulting in 'context-specific' or 'socially shaped' participatory practices (we return to this point a little further below). In the sections that follow we discuss the foregoing interconnected variants of participatory journalism in some detail.

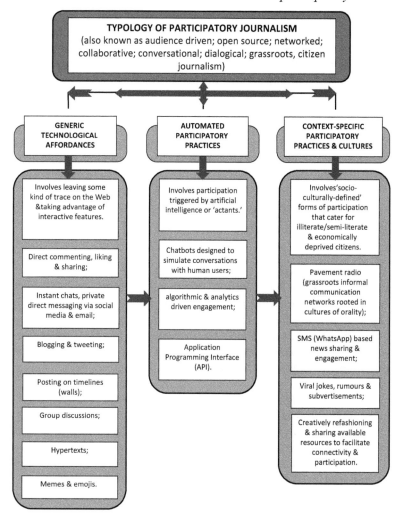

Figure 1.1 Interconnected variants of participatory journalism

Participation through generic technological affordances

In its simple and common forms, this form of participation involves users taking advantage of wide-ranging structural and *interactive features* embedded in digital technologies to leave 'some kind of trace on the web: a message, a comment, a like, a share, a vote etc.' (Olsson & Svensson 2012, 51). Although the participatory tools adopted by the media are continuously evolving, 'examples of this kind of participation are features like comments on the news, sending stories or pictures to the media, or sharing news on social networks using the options provided on the media website' (Suau & Pere 2014, 671). In this sense, *participatory journalism* 'encompasses all the interactions' audiences 'can have in the online environments provided by media' (Suau & Pere 2014, 671). Usher (2016) argues that from these developments

> [u]ser expectations for an online experience have grown in sophistication [...], in part due to user design enhancements (aided by coding advances and better understanding of how people move through the web [and its associated technologies], and in part due to a sophisticated online environment offering a rich, interactive environment for user exploration.
>
> (2016, 11)

This includes 'options [...] to respond, interact or even customise certain stories' (Deuze 2003, 206). As Westlund and Murschetz (2019, 58) observe, 'participatory journalism is a form of 'engaged' journalism in a hyper-connected media era that advocates for active audiences and community engagement. Under the participatory practices engendered by technologies, Olsson and Svensson (2012, 51) distinguish between three different levels of participation:

1   '*Active participation*', where the user initiates a discussion by posting a message.
2   '*Reactive participation*', where the user reacts to what is published by the producer and chooses to post a comment.
3   '*Promoted reactions*' where the user reacts to exhortations pronounced by the producer.

Whatever the nature of the participation, as some scholars contend, participatory journalism is 'most successful when [...] participation involves [some form of] *reciprocity or forms of relational exchange between professional journalists and audiences*/amateur news participants' (Wall 2017, 135, emphasis added). This entails moving from a closed journalistic culture with a focus on editorial content to an open journalistic culture with a focus on public connectivity and engagement (Deuze 2003). Wall submits that this open, two-way interactive reciprocity has been 'enhanced by the rise of social and other forms of online participatory media' (Wall 2017, 139) which provide users with both private chat/messaging platforms and public discussion boards, walls or timelines as well as group platform opportunities for participation. It is for this reason that scholars like Paterson (2013) restrict their definition of participatory journalism in Africa to '"social media" (blogging, tweeting and the like)' (2013, 1). Paterson further contends that the escalation in the use of these platforms to monitor and disseminate information has enabled African citizens to both bypass and influence traditional information flows, including mainstream news. In the African context, where mainstream media are generally inaccessible and often captured by the political and economic elites, participatory journalism provides an outlet for engaged citizenship.

Likewise, the mobile phone has also 'increasingly occupied a central position in discourses about participatory media in Africa' (Paterson 2013, 1), and there is abundant evidence showing that the technology is being used, to varying degrees, by citizens to contribute to newsmaking and information exchange in significant ways. Bivens, for example, observes that in Zimbabwe 'information sent from mobile phones makes up some of the only news coverage mainstream media organisations can acquire' (2008, 119). The SMS (short message service) is also seen as 'the dominant facilitator of new modes of participatory journalism in Africa' (Paterson 2013, 2). It is counted among the many technologies and platforms used by media organisations, particularly radio stations, to interact with audiences (Moyo, D. 2009).

Although *interactivity*, like other technological affordances, has evolved along with the Internet and its associated digital technologies, it remains a viable concept for understanding some of the basic technological affordances undergirding *participatory journalism* as a social practice in Africa and beyond. As Usher argues, it can be seen as some form of 'forward-looking innovation' adopted by news organisations following the realisation of 'the new [and inescapable] capacities for news creation [and consumption] enabled by advances in technology' (2016, 5). For some, it is seen as a 'defensive industry response' (p. 5) that has 'consequences for the [...] broader and more profound changes and redefinitions of professional journalism and its (news) culture as a whole' (Deuze 2003, 203).

Automated participatory practices

Rapid advances in the 'diffusion of computing processing, machine learning, algorithms, and data science' (Lewis 2015, 322) have spawned new developments and opportunities for participatory journalism which increasingly challenge and exert pressure on the agency of digital media users across the globe. These developments suggest that human and non-human actors are now increasingly at the centre of user engagement practices, and news organisations in Africa have not been spared the impact of the technological advancements. Although at relatively nascent stages in most sub-Saharan African countries, participatory practices structurally driven and shaped by developments in artificial intelligence (henceforth referred to as AI) such as algorithms, chatbots (automated robots), social bots and other communicative agents, are increasingly shaping online participatory cultures. The agents provide conversational output, and if commanded, can execute journalistic tasks, including enhancing audience experiences through influencing the course of online discussions and/or the opinions of readers. It is in this sense that the *actants* (non-human actors such as algorithms, chatbots etc.) have influenced user-participation practices in ways that demonstrate how the growing intersection between human and technological actors is complicating media audience interactions. However, because these *actants* are substrate, that is, they sit 'underneath the world as we experience it' (Drabinski 2018), they are deeply insidious and have, in some cases, been appropriated for the spread of fake news and cyberpropaganda. This explains why there have been calls for the auditing of algorithms and the development of ethical chatbots (Noble 2018; Kwet 2019).

These technologies have also been branded as agents of *digital or data colonialism* – a structural form of domination exercised through the centralised ownership and control of digital platforms through 'control over the flow of information [...] and a plethrora of other political [and] social functions' (Kwet 2019, 8). They do this through architectural designs that shape 'the rules, norms and behaviours of computer-mediated experiences in ways similar to architecture in physical space' (Kwet 2019, 8). Thus, while participatory practices emerging from these automated technical experiences are often blissfully conceived of as neutral, they are in fact infused with 'particular values and power relations' (Kwet 2019, 20). For example, algorithms are programmed to track and supply more of what users are looking for on digital media based on their location, past behaviours etc. resulting in users becoming 'more enscounced' in filter bubbles and encountering fewer and fewer alternative views (Markham 2017, 11). This has significant implications for shaping participatory practices 'because it cuts [users/readers] off from people with different views and interests [and] seriously undermines public deliberation' (Markham 2017, 11).

The era of automated journalism is also heavily linked to the strategic deployment and appropriations of editorial metric data in African media organisations. Because of the proliferation of social media analytic tools like Facebook Insights, Twitter Analytics, YouTube Analytics and Instagram Insights, media organisations can measure the performance of their news stories and assess the feedback from their audiences in real time (Carlson 2018). Media organisations have thus begun to use social media analytics to monitor, track and interact with their audiences. This trend has been characterised as signifying the rise of what Carlson (2018) has branded *measurable journalism* – 'the cultural and material shift to digital platforms capable of providing real-time, individualisable, quantitative data about audience consumption practices' (Carlson 2018, 409). This practice, as Moyo, D. et al. (2019, 492) contend, is 'associated with the shift to traceable news content that provides real-time quantitative data about audiences while permitting new modes of engagement and accountability'. It has become cheaper and easier for media organisations to automatically quantify likes, views, shares, comments and retweets on social media platforms. In this unfolding media environment, participation 'has become an engine of commerce [and] control' as well as 'new forms of cooptation and surveillance' (Barney et al. 2016, xxvii) by media organisations, governments as well as platform corporations.

Context-specific participatory practices and cultures

While the foregoing conceptions of *participatory journalism* are inextricably connected to advances in technology across both the Global North and the South, it is the context-specific factors that generate unique characteristics of participatory journalism in Africa. This reinforces the view that media 'professional identities are shaped and coloured by local factors' which spawn practices that 'challenge and throw into question the sweeping juggernaut and hegemony of Western professional ideologies, including the core principles and values that underpin the profession' (Mabweazara 2018, 1). Thus, although interactive digital technologies are imbued with 'preferred' participatory affordances as seen above, it is the situated users in their lived circumstances who creatively appropriate the technologies resulting in context-specific participatory practices that sometimes contradict platform-manufacturer-logic consequently setting elements of the African media scene apart from the scenario in the Global North. As Willems and Mano (2016, 4) argue, 'the experiences of audiences and engagements of users with a range of media […] are always grounded in particular contexts, worldviews and knowledge systems of life and wisdom'. They further contend that 'African media audiences and users *carry their contexts and cultural repertoires in the same way a tortoise carries its shell*' (Willems & Mano 2016, 4, emphasis added).

It is important, therefore, as we argue in this book, 'not to exaggerate the impact of digital media in having the ability to radically transform [...] audience experience' (Willems & Mano 2016, 9), especially given that in Africa, the notion of the 'digital divide' is well entrenched. Equally, it is important to recognise how local cultural values, innovations and creativity enable those with limited access and low digital literacy levels to engage with news content as well as participate in the news agenda. For example, local social media bundles (or what can be called partial Internet access) give rise to forms of participatory practices that differ markedly from those in areas with pervasive broadband Wi-Fi access. As Nyamnjoh (2005, 4) observes, this 'makes the African mediascape a rich and fascinating blend of traditions, influences and technologies. Coexisting in conviviality and interdependence are the most modern forms of communication technologies and indigenous media'. These hybrid realities underpin the nature and form of participatory journalism obtaining on the continent. To draw on Nyamnjoh (2005) again, it straddles 'the worlds of indigenous and modern media, creatively drawing on both to negotiate the communicative hurdles and hierarchies of the continent' (Nyamnjoh 2005, 218). Thus, within sub-Saharan Africa, participatory journalism needs to be seen as intricately interwoven with the broader socio-cultural, political and economic context, which shapes the way interactive digital technologies are appropriated.

In reminding us of the complexities of the African context, Goode (2009) submits that we should not forget the fact that in Africa, journalism has always existed alongside other unique forms of 'localised' news dissemination and storytelling practices. These include the popular creative deployment of technologies such as SMS and cartoons, as well as the generation of local unofficial communication practices such as *pavement sidewalk radio* also known as *radio trottoir*, which refers to the popular but 'unofficial discussions of current affairs' (Ellis 1989, 321), 'usually in the form of "anecdotal gossip"' (Nyamnjoh 2005, 218). This form of communication has proved effective not only as a vehicle for popular and informal discussion of power and current affairs [...] but also as a counter-power [...] often through the display of 'an extra ordinary verbal creativity rich in humour, parody and irony' (Nyamnjoh 2005, 218). Citing Ellis (1989), Nyamnjoh further argues that '*Africa's new press* shares many characteristics with *radio trottoir*, including identification with certain values, beliefs and outlooks commonly held by the population, some of which may appear bizarre and highly implausible to Western reporters and readers' (Nyamnjoh 2005, 218, emphasis added). This points to how communication practices, including the deployment of interactive digital technologies are enmeshed (and reimagined) in the heterogeneity of localised social interactions (Mabweazara 2015a). These dimensions of 'socially shaped' innovations; internal creativity and adaptations in Africa offer compelling evidence of the agency and creativity displayed by journalists and ordinary citizens in adopting and using new digital technologies (Mare 2014).

Considerations of the complexities of the 'contexts' in which African journalists operate also foregrounds the importance of attending to the intricacies of *local cultural factors*, which 'give credibility to additional theoretical ways' (Berger 2005, 1) of assessing how socially situated journalists are adjusting to the era of interactivity and participatory engagement. For example, the cultural orientation to communal values of *solidarity, interconnectedness* and *interdependence*, which 'focus our critical lenses to contingent social relationships and worldviews by which aspects of African journalism practice are maintained and defined' (Mabweazara 2015b, 115), highlight how citizens access digital technologies without necessarily being directly connected. In many situations, as Nyamnjoh (2005) argues, it suffices for an individual to be connected for whole groups and communities to benefit. Writing about the culture of mobile phone sharing in West Africa, Nyamnjoh posits that most mobile phone owners serve as a 'point of presence' in their communities, thus enabling those who cannot afford mobile phones to benefit from mobile phone services (Nyamnjoh 2005, 205).

An understanding of these *cultural dynamics* is central to our conceptualisation of participatory journalism in this book. These dynamics not only point us in the direction of the 'lived materialities of reportorial forms, practices and epistemologies' (Allan 2014, x), which show us where the potentials for participatory journalism in Africa are located, but also highlight where the challenges lie. As Willems and Mano (2016, 5) aptly advise, we need to consider the African continent 'as an epistemological location' that can be compared with insights emerging from other regions, especially the economically developed Global North.

To revert back to the existential question posed earlier: when exactly do participatory practices and cultures engendered by digital technologies, as seen in the three variants discussed above, *translate into journalism*? Our answer is simple: we submit that, when new interactive digital practices take centre stage and directly influence long-established journalistic cultures, albeit with some normative tensions and shifts, such practices inadvertently become a core part of journalism. They become 'the new normal', further extending the practice, materialisation and epistemology of journalism as a social construct. Thus, the act of liking, sharing, commenting and uploading images and videos, which shape and influence journalistic decision-making (and news content), inevitably become central to the practice of journalism in the 21st century.

Collectively, the above variants of participatory journalism speak directly to the increasingly prevalent notion of news *engagement* in the digital era, which runs across this book and is inherently connected to *participatory journalism* (Westlund & Murschetz 2019). Zelizer avers that 'the metaphor of engagement helps connect media outlets to journalism's longstanding objective of serving the public. It also *connects the news to impulses thought to engender involvement and connection across the digital environment*, news and non-news platforms alike' (2017, 23, emphasis added). This conception helps 'foment the linkage of news users to the non-news media at journalism's side, and in doing so it allows for a wider range of story forms' (Zelizer 2017, 23) as seen in the *context-specific participatory practices and cultures* discussed above and in Chapter 3. Zelizer further submits that at the very core of the notion of engagement 'rests the activity of sharing', which 'constitutes the primary act by which audiences experience news' in the era of *interactivity* and *virality* facilitated by social media and other digital platforms. A key point to note, however, as Zelizer rightly observes, is that although the notion of engagement 'was initially appended with the adjectives 'civic', 'public' or 'community' in earlier forms of journalism, today's notion of engagement does not always have that aspiration' (Zelizer 2017, 24), and this is certainly the case with our conception of 'engagement' in this book.

Overarching theoretical orientation and methods

While belief in the transformative power of the Internet and its closely associated interactive technologies still implicitly underpin much of the thinking on their potential implications for African journalism, 'the brazen techno-euphoric moment of wonderment and awe characteristic of the mid-1990s no longer occupies mainstream thought on the Internet in Africa' (Mabweazara 2017, 405). After realising the shortcomings of exclusively apportioning 'power' to digital technologies, contemporary scholarship has warily shifted to cautious positions sensitive to the complexities and contradictions that mediate the appropriation of the technologies in various social sectors. A corpus of research that critically examines the shifting ecology of African journalism and how it is adjusting to the changing structurations of society has emerged (see Paterson 2013; Mare 2014). This research emphasises the 'situated nature' of digital technologies in journalism practice, especially the influences of localised socio-political, economic and cultural circumstances in which the technology is assimilated and *appropriated*. It questions the *technicist* inclinations of early scholarship and maintains a critical alertness to the *social shaping* nature of technology. As Conboy (2013, 149) reminds us, 'Technology, in isolation, has never made journalism better or worse [... It] does not drive change. It has to adapt to the patterns of cultural expectation within particular societies at specific moments in time'.

In this line of thought, the imperatives shaping African journalism in the digital era are seen as 'negotiated in converging circumstances of economic, political and cultural factors' (Allan 2014, ix), all ordinarily seen as commonsensical. This 'critical sociological turn' acknowledges and considers the 'localised' socio-cultural, political and economic realities which shape adoption practices as well as uses of digital technologies by journalists in Africa. These localised conditions also point to the lasting setbacks associated with the realities of 'access' to digital technologies, thus foregrounding crucial questions of *structure* and *agency* (Mare 2014; Mabweazara 2017). In the light of the foregoing conceptual and theoretical shifts, this book also shuns deterministic approaches and reinvigorates traditional and critical sociological approaches to both journalism and technology which collectively see the adoption of interactive and participatory digital practices in (African) journalism as shaped by complex contextual factors that structure journalists' attitudes, adoption practices and appropriations. Thus, to understand the impact of new digital technologies on journalism practice in Africa, we must put journalists into a critical analytical context and begin to question the immediate and wider social context in which they deploy technologies (Mabweazara 2011; Mare 2014). This approach finds root in the collective strengths of two broad theoretical concerns: the *sociology of journalism* and *social constructivist approaches to technology*. Although these theoretical bodies were conceptualised before the 'new media age' – in the 1970s and 80s – together they provide a basis for conceptualising the interplay between journalists, their everyday practice and the wider social factors that coalesce to structure and constrain the deployment of new technologies (Pinch & Bijker 1984).

The early newsroom studies that crystallised in the *sociology of journalism* offer enduring insights into the working practices of journalists and thus provide a 'default setting' against which most news production studies have been rooted. As Paterson (2008, 2) contends, without these 'early ethnographic investigations of news production, our understandings of journalism would be limited to what little we are able to glean from the observation of news content, or from what journalists say they do'. Similarly, social constructivist approaches to technology, which emphasise the social shaping and 'interpretive flexibility' of technology offer a frame in which technologies can be understood as not necessarily replacing existing social realities and dynamics in which they are appropriated, but rather as continuous with and embedded in them (Bijker 1995; Pinch & Bijker 1984). In the context of this book, these approaches help us to understand digital participatory practices as 'socially constructed multifaceted' realities rather than as monolithic experiences that impose their 'own logic [... on] media companies' (Domingo 2008, 19).

In deploying these influential theoretical frameworks, we therefore acknowledge that journalism (and research into journalism) is not performed in a vacuum, independent of the shaping impact of contextual influences. This chimes with *structuration theory*, which 'refuse[s] to afford either technology or society a deterministic role, but view[s] technology and society in interaction' (Wasserman 2011, 156). Extending this argument further, Mare (2014, 12) argues that the disruptive impact of digital technologies needs to be understood as a 'duality of influences' – the *human agency* of individual journalists and owners (internal newsroom creativity) vis-à-vis the *wider context* of news production (restructuring of journalism practice). In this sense, the intricacies of digital participatory practices in Africa are seen as socially and culturally shaped.

Methodologically, we extensively draw our empirical evidence from a longitudinal qualitative exploratory approach involving the use of multiple cases (newsrooms and key informants), as well as data collection procedures, including participant and non-participant observation (online and offline); in-depth interviews (online, telephonically as well as in-situ within newsrooms); qualitative content analysis; and document analysis to offer a mix of 'thick descriptions' and 'insider' perspectives of interactive participatory practices and cultures emerging across a range of sub-Saharan African newsroom and media contexts in countries that include Mozambique, South Africa, Namibia, Zambia, Zimbabwe, Kenya and Uganda, among others. This approach enabled us to examine the intricately connected variants of 'participatory journalism' as discussed above (see Figure 1.1) in an overarching exploratory trajectory that allowed us to capture the dynamic technological evolution from the SMS to emergent technologies like editorial analytics, algorithms, chatbots and AI. The expansive nature of research enabled studying the same news organisations and contexts (online and offline) several times in an iterative process that stretched between 2008 and 2020. This longitudinal approach allowed us to track the critical moments in the metamorphosis of participatory journalism in sub-Saharan Africa over an extended period of time.

The online exploratory fieldwork included an immersive digital ethnography, observation and analysis of different news organisations' user comment sections and social media platforms. In adopting this methodological approach, we followed McKenna et al.'s (2017, 87) advice that social media 'provides qualitative researchers with a new window into [the] outer and inner worlds' of individual and institutional social experiences. They further submit that '[t]here is literally a flood of qualitative data [...] on Twitter, Facebook [...], all of which can be downloaded, interpreted, and analysed'. Following this advice, we carefully selected screenshots as well as textual data from a range of publicly available posts on social media pages run by news media organisations in order to 'increase the contextual understanding of the reader [and] provide empirical evidence to support [theoretical arguments]' (McKenna et al. 2017, 92). In total, we interviewed over 150 journalists across a range of sub-Saharan African countries. Our key informants included online managers, editors and webmasters all of whom possessed information and insights that facilitated an understanding of the ongoing interactions between news organisations and their immediate and wider context of practice.

Overall, the research approach we adopted enabled us to capture the dynamics of how newsrooms (and their journalists) are embracing digital participatory practices, including readers' comments as part of their everyday newsmaking cultures, and the resulting professional and ethical dilemmas.

How the book is organised

We have broadly organised the chapters in this book around the previously discussed variants of participatory journalism, which, as we have argued, collectively define participatory journalism in Africa. The four core chapters that follow reflect these larger conceptual themes. Although some of these chapters deal with specific technologies in isolation, in exploring the participatory practices and cultures that develop around them, we broadly take a communicative ecological approach that considers the interrelationships and overlaps among the different technologies. As we have argued, a basic assumption throughout the chapters is that the appropriation of digital media reflects and also shapes the social context in which they are deployed.

Following the overarching overview provided in this introductory chapter, Chapter 2 explores online comments – one of the most pragmatic and influential attributes of the digital era in Africa. We specifically look at how leading print newsrooms are adapting to the wave of changes spawned by readers' comments on their news websites and social media platforms, and how journalists are handling the 'new' context in which strangers contribute and respond directly to something they alone once controlled. In doing this, we also consider the professional dilemmas emerging with the volumes of user generated content (UGC) posted on interactive platforms and the approaches taken in managing and 'gatekeeping' the content. The lack of clear gatekeeping strategies, as we discuss further in Chapter 5, has opened floodgates of abuse, hate speech and extremist views that pose serious threats to the core values and normative ideals of traditional journalism.

In Chapter 3, we consider how the intersection between a range of social media platforms and user participatory cultures is shaping news production and consumption practices. As well as foregrounding the revitalisation of grassroots informal communication networks such as 'pavement radio', we argue that solicited and unsolicited audience participation and engagement through social media platforms are not only reshaping news production practices and cultures in resource constrained environments but also recalibrating the ways in which news is shared, consumed and recycled across multiple platforms. The chapter demonstrates several ways in which various social media platforms are being used to varying degrees in ways that directly implicate newsmaking and information exchange across a range of African countries.

Chapter 4 examines participatory journalism in the age of rapid advances in AI, computing processing, machine learning, chatbots and algorithms. Recent developments suggest that human and non-human actors are at the centre of user engagement practices, and news organisations in Africa have not been spared from these developments, especially on social media platforms. The chapter unpacks the extent to which chatbots and algorithms are an issue in Africa and the implications they have for online participatory cultures. We note that besides enhancing customer experiences and supporting user interface, *actants* like algorithms and chatbots have been used in South Africa, Zimbabwe, South Africa, Nigeria and Kenya to spread rumours and misinformation or attack people for posting their opinions online, hence calling for auditing algorithms and the development of ethical chatbots.

Chapter 5 examines the dilemmas facing news organisations and their journalists as they adjust to the ever-evolving era of digital participatory practices. It specifically looks at how the appropriation of interactive digital technologies has contributed to a transformation of journalism at a number of levels, including news sourcing routines, audience engagement and the structuring of the working day. The chapter also highlights how the era of digital interactivity has spawned a number of localised ethical dilemmas that border around *copyright infringements*; the proliferation of *misinformation, mal-information and disinformation*; the *invasion of personal privacy*; the *institutionalisation and normalisation of filter bubbles* and the proliferation of *hate speech* and *online harassment*, among other issues. We also discuss how news organisations are making efforts to moderate UGC on their interactive spaces.

In Chapter 6, we pull together the broader argument of the book by foregrounding the changing nature of user participation cultures and practices in different African journalistic contexts. We also reflect on how interactive participatory practices point to the shifting ontological foundations of journalism as inherently *participatory*, although developments in AI increasingly challenge and exert pressure on the agency of media users. We conclude by cautioning against attempts to flatten a wide range of experiences under one banner – Africa. As the book broadly shows, there are many nuances and experiences across the continent that are impossible to capture in the space available in this book.

2 Readers' comments

How audiences' voices are challenging and (re)defining traditional journalism

The Web 2.0 era has revolutionised readers' participation and engagement with the news in hitherto unseen ways. As noted in the previous chapter, the participatory cultures emerging with interactive digital technologies are offering myriad opportunities for readers to participate and interact with the news. In particular, readers' online comments are proving to be a popular form of participatory journalism, giving readers 'agency [and] authority to influence newsmaking' (Hermida 2011a, 14). While in the past, the participation of readers was limited to radio phone-in programmes and letters-to-the-editor in newspapers, readers' online comments have become almost ubiquitous, providing one of the most pragmatic and influential attributes of the interactive functionality of the digital era. As Reich tells us: 'No other forum has been so open, offering such an immediate and unedited access to any citizen wishing to express a view about specific news as it unfolds' (2011, 113).

However, the implications of user comments for traditional journalism in Africa have received limited scholarly attention. While a sizeable amount of research on participatory practices and cultures has emerged mainly from Western scholarship (see Hermida 2011a, 2011b; Singer et al. 2011; Usher 2016; Wall 2017), empirical evidence on emerging practices in Africa and the wider Global South is generally lacking. This research lacuna has often meant that developments in African journalism are all too often measured against the backdrop of Western advances (professional and otherwise); this tends to overlook local idiosyncrasies and contextual factors that shape and underlie journalistic cultures in Africa. These factors include the socio-political, economic and institutional contexts that are markedly different from those in the West – often less clear-cut and resistant to any attempts to simplify them.

This chapter, therefore, seeks to contribute an African perspective on how mainstream journalists are embracing readers' online comments.

It draws its empirical evidence from leading print newsrooms – mainly from Zimbabwe's dominant state-controlled Zimbabwe Newspapers Group (Zimpapers) and the small but powerful privately owned Alpha Media Holdings (AMH) – to examine how journalists are adapting and adjusting to the participatory cultures and UGC associated with online readers' comments. The chapter specifically explores how the newsrooms (and their journalists) are embracing readers' comments as part of their everyday newsmaking cultures, as well as the resulting professional and ethical concerns. It also examines the newsrooms' approaches to managing and 'gatekeeping' the comments.

Online readers' comments: A brief overview of emerging theoretical observations

Although readers' comment forums on newspaper websites are still heavily under-researched, there is a general consensus among scholars that they have become one of the most pragmatic and influential attributes of the online era (Hermida 2011b; Reich 2011; Santana 2011; Singer et al. 2011; Ksiazek & Springer 2020). As spontaneous, informal, and predominantly anonymous public forums, they represent a 'new opinion pipeline not seen in the letters-to-the-editors section of the printed newspaper' (Santana 2011, 77).

Researchers have focused on a number of areas that point to the growing significance of readers' comments on online platforms. One line of enquiry has examined how comments are revolutionising traditional newsroom norms and practices by augmenting and reinventing the means by which they interact with their readers and sources, as well as the way readers interact and relate with one another (McElroy 2013). The interactivity and connections facilitated by user comments are seen as enabling journalists to access information, ideas and feedback from their readers in ways that differ markedly from the 'arms-length' operations of traditional mass media (McElroy 2013; Milioni et al. 2012). Scholars argue that the surge in user-led sharing and discussion of news stories allows journalists to gather first-hand material, especially if they are physically remote from the scenes and issues raised by the readers (Gulyas 2013). Gulyas further observes that participatory platforms can enhance the degree of authenticity in stories, as they take 'journalists closer to [news sources] where the [stories are] actually happening' (2013, 272). In this sense, the comment forums are seen as 'expand[ing] the range of participants available to engage in news [production]' (Bruns and Highfield 2012, 21).

Research into user comments is often connected to general discussions on generic affordances of interactive digital technologies and their impact on the practices and cultures of online journalism. Writing at the turn of the century, Pavlik observed that the era of interactive and participatory cultures has seen the emergence of a 'two-way symmetric model of communication [in which] the flow of communication is […] much more a dialog between […] parties to communication' (2000, 235–236). Pavlik conceived interactivity as bringing about a shift in relationships between news organisations and their publics. This view is echoed from an African perspective by Moyo, D. (2009) in his observation that the ability to engage with news and with other news consumers is giving African readers greater influence over the material covered in newspapers while at the same time providing journalists with an opportunity to access ideas and leads from the readers.

For some, the participatory culture of interactive digital technologies is seen as giving readers 'the power to challenge professional media mono-poly by setting the agenda and framing the news' (Milioni et al. 2012, 23). Bruns argues that through readers' comments, the initial news reports are 'fleshed out, examined, critiqued, debunked, put into context, and linked with other news, events and background information'. This process 'externalizes and turns [news] into a widely distributed collaborative effort […] which previously took place either entirely within the minds of active news consumers, or within small relatively isolated groups of consumers discussing the news of the day' (Bruns 2008, 178). It is in this context that Singer et al. (2011, 1) postulate that: 'The twenty-first-century newspaper is essentially never complete, neither finished nor finite […]. Nor are journalists the only ones determining what gets recorded. A great many other people also contribute content, representing their own interests, ideas, observations and opinions'.

This direct participation and engagement by readers is also tied to online comments' deliberative potential, which some scholars see as enabling citizens to challenge and monitor traditional journalistic discourse by 'acting as watchdogs of the watchdogs' (Milioni et al. 2012, 23). In the same manner, citizens are seen as directly con-fronting topics avoided by the mainstream media in contexts where editorial and political constraints weigh down on the practice of professional journalism (Frere 2014).

Researchers have also focused on the negative implications of online readers' comments. In particular, the underlying logic of 'openness and participation' (Lewis 2012, 840) characteristic of the comment forums is seen as challenging traditional editorial 'gatekeeping' standards (Hermida 2011b). This has led to concerns about the anonymity, lack of civility and unruliness of comment sections (McElroy 2013; Ksiazek & Springer 2020), what Quandt (2018) broadly refers to as 'dark forms of participation'. For Reich (2011, 104), 'writing under pennames lowers both the "intellectual level" of comments and user responsibility for them'. Comments are reduced to 'random rants which are neither policed nor engaged with by journalistic or editorial staff' (Bruns & Highfield 2012, 17).

These drawbacks, which have resulted in a growing number of news organisations abandoning commenting features altogether (Ksiazek & Springer 2020), are directly linked to the burden of moderating user comments. As Singer et al. (2011, 3) argue: '[w]hen journalism becomes 'participatory', the volume of transmitted information rapidly surges to flood levels, swamping traditional approaches to winnowing and the like'. Bruns further submits that in the interactive digital era, 'gatekeeping' 'as a means of ensuring broad and balanced coverage' is no longer strictly necessary as the 'gates have multiplied beyond all control' (2008, 176).

Beyond the foregoing dilemmas, some researchers observe that journalists' dependence on UGC in news reporting portends a decline in 'originality' as the readily available information generated online encourages journalists to become 'data consumers rather than creators' (Peters 2011, 155). Locating this argument in the African context, where access to the Internet is predominantly disproportionate, Mabweazara (2013) argues that journalists' reliance on online information for story ideas tends to narrow their perspective. In his view, individuals who actively contribute to comment threads 'command the discursive field and set the agenda for issues' (2013, 143) covered by reporters, much to the annihilation of potential voices without the means or ability to effectively engage with or contribute to the discourses circulating on the forums.

Researchers have also questioned the one-sided nature of deliberations on comment forums. Canter, for example, notes that while the nature of participation on comment threads is an interactive one, it is mainly between readers 'rather than being between readers and journalists' (2013, 615). She contends that while journalists 'may be willing to let readers respond to, and interact with, already produced material [...], they are less willing to give them any real influence over the news process by engaging or collaborating' (p. 605). Milioni et al. (2012, 21) similarly argues that, 'whereas users challenge journalistic viewpoints to some extent, this type of audience participation is not likely to render audiences co-producers of news content in significant ways'. For this reason, traditional mainstream media are largely seen as retaining their control over content and participation on user comment forums (Reich 2011; Canter 2013).

The adoption of readers' online comments: The case of Zimbabwean print newsrooms

While most newspapers in Africa assumed an online presence in the late 1990s and have always devoted space for letters-to-the-editor, in Zimbabwe newsrooms were generally slow in seizing the opportunities for audience interaction afforded by the Internet. For several years the Zimbabwean mainstream press did not prioritise interactivity on their newspaper websites. As elsewhere, the adoption of commenting functions was 'a product of trial and error' (Reich 2011, 97) as news organisations stubbornly steered users to more traditional channels. However, around 2007 following international trends and practices that emerged with news websites established by exiled Zimbabwean journalists, the privately owned AMH's newspapers took the lead in the adoption of readers' comments (Mabweazara 2011). The media house refurbished and furnished all its newspapers' websites with interactive features that enable readers to comment and contribute content directly to the newspapers (Mabweazara 2014). Explaining the reasoning behind these developments, AMH's Editor-in-Chief at the time rhapsodised: 'We are upping our game to ensure that we don't disappoint our readers who are yearning for lively commentary and *groundbreaking open journalism in which readers are not mere audiences, but active participants in content sourcing and formulating debate* (emphasis added)'.[1]

This transition marked a key stage in the adoption of participatory journalism in Zimbabwe. The interactive features of newspaper websites represented a marked 'cultural' shift from the tightly controlled participatory antecedents such as letters-to-the-editors, rooted in the traditional top-down approach to news production, especially in the state-controlled press. By allowing audiences into the 'previously closed world of journalism' (Hermida 2011b, 178), an avalanche of comments and discussions from readers of all socio-political dispositions scattered across the globe flooded the news websites. Unlike the letters-to-the-editor, online comments made it possible to present, within the same edition, readers' reactions to stories as well as to each other's comments. Thus, journalists found themselves in a new professional context where the previously distant connections with readers and sources had collapsed.

After an initial period of resistance and in-house tensions, in 2010 the state-controlled Zimpapers followed in the footsteps of AMH by overhauling its newspapers' websites to incorporate interactive features (Mabweazara 2014). Although Zimpapers' slow adoption of interactive digital platforms was also linked to the prolonged economic challenges faced by the country after the turn of the century, an entrenched culture of conservatism and concerns about how the public was likely to respond to its well-known partisan editorial content also played a key part in the delays (Zimpapers is generally perceived as blatantly partisan in its support for the ruling party, the Zimbabwe African National Union – Patriotic Front (ZANU-PF) (Moyo, D. 2009).

The radical shift from a deep-rooted conservative 'top-down' news culture in which readers' voices were traditionally addressed in a tokenistic fashion via the letters-to-the-editor clearly demonstrated what Peters (2011, 155) refers to as the fear of 'court[ing] obscurity and potential irrelevance' by disregarding the changes and dynamics ushered in by the era of interactive digital technologies. As Zimpapers' Group Online Editor explained: 'The changes in the media industry the world over cannot be ignored [...] times are changing. It's clear people want their input [...] considered. The changes were inevitable [...]. *We just had to move with the times*' (emphasis added). This view reinforces Wall's (2017) observation that in the era of interactive digital technologies, participatory journalism can be seen as introducing 'the idea that citizens have a right to a news narrative' (2017, 137) that can challenge and decentre dominant news discourses.

Although both AMH and Zimpapers had divergent approaches and motives to adopting interactivity, in 2011 they both created new job profiles which led to the recruitment of Group Online Editors. These roles were entrusted with evolving responsibilities, which included 'repurposing print content for the web; using social media to engage and deliver content to their audiences; as well as filtering User Generated Content' on newspaper websites and social media platforms (Mabweazara 2013, 137). These new roles worked closely with senior editorial staff in ensuring that the digital platforms of each newspaper reflect the editorial thrust of the news organisation as well as cultivating an enriching user experience. Thus, while the news organisations can broadly be seen as adjusting to online operational procedures, the structures in place across both institutions indicate 'transition and adaptation to the era of interactivity and participatory digital journalism' (Mabweazara 2014, 67). The rest of the chapter explores the wide-ranging ways in which audiences' voices on these news organisations' newspaper websites are redefining traditional ways of doing journalism.

Readers' comments as alternative channels for feedback and story ideas

Despite the fact that both AMH and Zimpapers newsrooms are still generally figuring out how to 'normalise' readers' comments into their established day-to-day practices, there was a general consensus among journalists that this interactive and participatory culture is increasingly moving centre stage, thus shaping and contributing to the dynamics of newsmaking in the newsrooms. Journalists across newsrooms found readers' comments useful, and generally noted that even with the challenges embedded in embracing readers' voices, they still offered critical insights that informed editorial processes and decisions. In addition to providing fodder for story ideas, some of which became exclusives, readers' comments were seen as helping journalists to connect with readers, 'even if this entail[ed] setting aside time to sift through tons of dross', as one news editor put it.

Readers' comments were thus viewed as complementing the wider ecology of resources at the journalists' disposal in gathering insights and feedback from their readers. Journalists across news beats highlighted that they had 'ritualised' the reading of comments to their stories. As one desk editor at Zimpapers' *Chronicle* explained: 'It is always interesting to engage with readers' responses to one's stories [...], *in fact, it has become part of my ritual every morning*' (emphasis added). For most journalists, this 'ritualisation' of readers' comments was hinged on the platforms' potential to provide useful feedback and insights into the popular mood and sentiments in response to news content and broader socio-political issues. A senior reporter at AMH's *NewsDay* explained thus: 'the feedback helps me gather ideas about how people feel, which is crucial for my next article. It helps my understanding of the type [...] of news people are looking for'. This embedding of readers' comments into journalists' everyday routines points to an emerging *normative routine*, which underpins the way journalists generate and construct their stories, as one reporter at *The Standard* (AMH) succinctly put it:

> [...] it is not satisfying anymore to write a story that does not trigger a flurry of comments. You sort of write your story with that in mind. You want readers to engage with your story [...], but equally you're sort of petrified by what is likely to follow.

Journalists further noted that in some cases comments corrected misnomers and factual inaccuracies or even altered their outlook on the newsworthiness of a story. A senior business reporter at *The Zimbabwe Independent* (AMH) gave a lucid explanation: 'We don't always get things right [...] some comments are useful because readers point to shortcomings in the way we cover stories, and this can be useful for improving the quality of our product, disconcerting as it sounds'.

While journalists retained the power to decide which ideas to pursue, readers' comments were perceived as broadening their purview by 'nudging them towards new and different ways to tell stories' (Santana 2011, 77). The influence of readers' comments in newsmaking processes also spilled into editorial meetings. Participants in the study highlighted that senior editors increasingly evoked issues raised on comment threads in editorial conferences, often cautioning reporters or pointing to issues that required follow-ups. As one reporter at *The Standard* put it: 'Time without number our Editor-in-Chief mentions readers' feedback in our editorial meetings, which riles most of us. Often there are warnings about the dangers of being sued, poor sourcing or even embarrassing grammatical errors'. This development further points to readers' voices increasingly taking centre stage in shaping the news agenda of the newspapers. Although journalists remain in control of the news process, they can no longer claim exclusive access to 'the truth', as news has become an open-ended 'artefact', subject to challenge and ongoing critique by a readership that offers multiple perspectives and responses from a variety of angles and experiences.

Although the integration of audience voices has not qualitatively tempered with the basic values and principles of journalism, the interactivity of news websites is enabling journalists to harness 'the collective intelligence and knowledge' of dedicated users who 'filter the news flow' (Bruns 2008, 176–177) by highlighting and debating salient topics of importance to them. In the words of Bruns (2008, 178), user comments are turning news 'from a relatively static product to be consumed by audiences into a dynamic, evolving, expanding resource that is *actively co-developed by the users*' (emphasis added). We are therefore witnessing an ecological reconfiguration and recasting of dimensions of news production in ways that echo Sigal's 1970s observation that 'News organisations [...] alter their procedures, and [...] make innovative responses to [...] novel situations' (1973, 101).

Although questions of 'access' to the Internet and users' abilities to contribute meaningfully to online deliberations have a potential to skew news agendas (see Chapter 5), the anonymity and distributed nature of voices that comment on stories was interpreted as considerably swaying journalists away from their tradition of sourcing news (and comments) from the same elite sources. A senior business reporter at Zimpapers' *Sunday News* aptly summed up this point: 'The people who always come to our mind are professionals or well-known figures, *but with online comments it's different, anyone with his facts right can throw in their opinion* (emphasis added)'. Explaining this point further, a senior reporter at *NewsDay* stated:

Engaging with readers' comments allows one to explore or think of several aspects of a story [...]. Angles to the story may be as many as the number of positions occupied by people with an interest in the issue at stake. *Readers' comments, when they are useful, help to reveal some of these angles, which can be initially overlooked* [...].

(emphasis added)

These findings reinforce Pavlik's (2000, 235–236) observation at the turn of the century on the emergence of a multipronged model of communication in which the flow of information is becoming much more of a shared 'dialog between [...] all parties to communication'. This is a particularly important development, especially in contexts where information flows are generally restricted or censored such as in Zimbabwe (Moyo, D. 2009). By appropriating readers' comments, journalists are, therefore, strategically locating themselves at *the source*, 'where information is most likely to flow to them' (Sigal 1973, 11).

Deliberative engagement and participatory cultures on comment threads

Beyond the direct professional implications discussed above, readers' online comments were also seen as embodying spaces of 'unfettered' public deliberation, which, in the terms of the journalists, 'complement', 'extend', 'enrich' as well as 'tear apart' news discourses. Comments were described as sometimes generating hard-hitting alternative discourses that confronted issues deliberately avoided by news organisations in Zimbabwe. In the words of one senior journalist at the state-controlled Zimpapers' *Herald*:

Hardcore political discussion has shifted to the online forums [...]. Readers have taken it in their own hands to create their own narrative and provide the other side of the story. As you and I know, there is a limit to the issues that newspapers in Zimbabwe can write about [...]

Several journalists across the divide of the state-controlled Zimpapers and privately owned AMH explicitly described readers' comment forums as potentially fulfilling a deliberative role akin to the Habermasian notion of the public sphere, a normative ideal long-lost in the morass of restrictive editorial policies and the general tight control and regulation of the media in the country (Moyo, D. 2009). A senior editor at *NewsDay* aptly explained this point:

These forums are abuzz with very critical commentary on the state's leadership, fiscal policy, land reform issues, and police brutality [...]. The critical issues that concern Zimbabweans, but which are not easily accommodated on our pages because of government censorship and harsh reactions to negative or critical publicity.

In the limited mainstream spaces for critical deliberations, especially on political issues, online comment forums were seen as a central place for citizens to exchange views on wide-ranging socio-political issues, especially when they offer a substantial amount of factual information or, as McElroy (2013, 756) puts it, demonstrate 'a public process of weighing alternatives via the expression of issue positions and supporting rationales'. Accone (2000, 69) further adds that the anonymous nature of online interactions 'encourages debate. The kind of discourse that would never grace the [printed pages of newspapers], because users are comfortable expressing themselves freely under the guise of non-traceable nom de plumes'.

While readers' online comments are triggered by professionally generated news stories they are, however, seen as offering alternative discourses that challenge and sometimes usurp journalists' position as 'agenda setters of public discourses [and] watchdogs of society', as one reporter at the *Chronicle* put it. For many journalists, the multiple voices that comment on stories online 'bridge' the polarised editorial content in Zimbabwe's mainstream media by offering an alternative 'balancing act' to partisan news discourses. The heterogeneity of voices and points of view online are seen as challenging the hierarchies of discourses in news stories. This complex intersection between news discourses and readers' comments in the formation of public opinion was described by a senior reporter at *The Standard*:

> In a significant number of comments, readers tend to challenge our viewpoints [...] including the sources we use [...]. They also take each other to task, and this has far-reaching implications for the reader as it culminates in 'new hybrid texts' that collectively shape meanings on critical public issues.

This observation chimes with Bruns' remark that comment forums 'offer a corrective, an alternative interpretation of [issues] by adding the backstory and providing further related (and often contradicting) information enabling readers to better assess for themselves and by themselves the quality and veracity of mainstream news stories' (Bruns 2008, 177). Thus, while the news media in Zimbabwe are heavily polarised and partisan, the same news online is open to a higher degree of contestation than is typical of traditional news media (Bruns 2008; Fenton 2010).

However, journalists highlighted that while readers' comments were useful on several fronts as discussed above, they hardly engaged directly with readers on the platforms – for them, the idea of 'entering into a substantive exchange' (Hermida 2011b, 181) of views with readers is not yet part of their mindset. This points to two issues: *first*, that Zimbabwean newsrooms, as elsewhere in Africa, are still broadly adjusting to the culture of interactivity, including figuring out ways of actively engaging with readers in the true spirit of participatory and interactive journalism. As AHM's group online editor explained: 'we are still exploring ways of engaging directly with readers without distorting the flow of the discourses on these forums [...] At the moment we are leaving everything to the readers, let them determine the nature of the interactions'. This response relates to Frere's (2014, 250) observations that journalists 'are uncertain as to whether they should enter into a new type of relationship with their public' in keeping with the cultures and practices emerging with technological changes in their newsrooms.

Secondly, and interpreted differently, the lack of direct interactions between journalists and readers can also be seen as 'rooted in long-established power dynamics' or imbalances (Hermida 2011b, 180) which reduce online comments to 'listening devices [rather than] devices for a dialogue between journalists and audiences' (2011b, 181). Consequently, it could be argued that the dynamics of participation in *invited spaces of participation* like comments sections are not only dependent on 'whose rules of the game are used to determine who enters the space' (Gaventa 2006, 60), but also on the 'silent rules' or ingrained etiquette that shapes the nature and form of participation once in the interactive space. For this reason, terms like '*permitted reactive participation*' (Olsson & Svensson 2012), '*mediated quasi-interaction*' (Thompson 2020) or '*minimalist forms of participation*' (Carpentier 2011) can be more appropriate descriptors of the deliberative engagements and participatory cultures on readers' comment sections. In short, as Carpentier (2011) avers, participation on comments sections is not always necessarily *participatory, bottom-up* and *open* because journalists and their newsrooms 'set the frames' and parameters for the conversations and thus foster what some scholars have referred to as an '*interactive illusion*' (Jönsson & Örnebring 2011). This observation further finds support in Reich's view that 'comments leave the journalist in the traditional position of the lead singer, while audience members generally play the minor, faceless and reactive role of the chorus' (2011, 98).

Some journalists, however, attributed the lack of direct interactions with readers to the widespread use of pseudonyms and anonymity on comment forums, which made it difficult to generate useful dialogue. This marked a clear distinction with journalists' use of other interactive platforms such as social media, especially Facebook, which provided scope for building direct intimate connections with readers and potential sources (see Mabweazara 2014). Consequently, the most direct form of journalists' engagement with readers' comments was in the moderation of the content. This echoes Singer's 2009 observation at *The New York Times* in which she contends that comment forums were reactive places that did not include journalists beyond simply 'monitoring for abuse' (2009, 481).

The lack of policy directions on whether journalists should engage directly with readers' comments for both the state controlled (Zimpapers) and private newsrooms (AMH) was also raised as a key impediment. However, some veteran journalists across the divide emphasised the importance of adhering to the key journalistic ethos of *detachment* and *impartiality* by not actively participating in online deliberations. One reporter explained thus: 'There is a risk of exposing your personal ideological position or emotions if you engage directly with these comments [...]. As you know, we should always be seen to be impartial and balanced'. This 'rigid' application of traditional normative values in online practices further indicates a shift to the web with a deeply ingrained 'legacy media' mindset that 'permanently' consigns readers to the position of 'audiences for journalistic work' (Reich 2011, 102).

Normative threats and pressures to longstanding journalistic norms

Although readers' comments are broadly positively transforming the news media ecosystem and culture in Zimbabwe, they are, however, not without negative implications or threats to established practices and cultures. As Canter (2013, 604) observes in the context of British local newspapers, the 'rise in participatory journalism has led to new challenges for journalists as they [strive] to negotiate the often-murky waters of user-generated content'. In our study, journalists pointed to a number of unsettling individual concerns as well as generic ethical and professional dilemmas emerging with hosting audience voices on their newspaper websites. While most of these concerns related to well-known challenges associated with the interactive and participatory cultures of the digital era (see detailed discussion in Chapter 5), in the Zimbabwean context, some of the issues were tied to local contextual factors, especially the consequences of opening up communicative spaces to an *embittered public* that has endured years of a closed media environment and a harsh economic environment.

A number of concerns were raised by hardliners among senior journalists who described the permeation of readers' voices into their routine practices as akin to ceding their journalistic 'power' to a mass of unqualified ordinary citizens who 'have, in fact, become de facto "watchdogs" of [their] professional activities', as one veteran reporter at the *Chronicle* put it. The journalists generally felt uneasy with this new dynamic and pointed to its potential impact on their personal morale and confidence as professionals. A key concern was around the influence of readers' comments on performance evaluations within newsrooms, especially for journalists whose work was persistently subjected to the harsh scrutiny of readers. As one assistant business editor at Zimpapers' flagship *The Herald* explained: 'Some comments are [...] downright degrading and personal. In your mind you're thinking, *"if the editor-in-chief sees this, then I'm in for a thorough hiding"* [...]. *It can be quite distressing*' (emphasis added). Particular concern was raised about how some comments were seen as challenging 'the professional's' journalistic integrity in disconcerting ways. As one reporter explained:

> A lot of people now rely on our websites. They post comments and do all sorts of things with our news product. *If you lie or get your facts wrong, readers will take you to the cleaners. And editors are becoming very strict. If they see queries [...] or negative comments about your story they'll send the feedback to you and you have to account for it [...]*.
>
> (emphasis added)

From the above, it is clear that readers' comments are not only threatening journalists' 'traditional position of influence and importance' (Bruns 2008, 173) but also indirectly propping up a sense of professional vigilance and responsibility by directly criticising their work.

Beyond the above personal worries, journalists described some comments as careless expressions of frustration and anger with the country's politics and economy without adding any qualitative value to the subject of the stories. Explaining this challenge, AMH's group online editor stated: 'We often say, just joking with colleagues in the newsroom, that [...] [t]here is so much anger [among Zimbabweans] online, and this manifests in unwarranted personal attacks'. This concern relates to

Frere's observations about the 'the bitter citizen' in Burkina Faso who uses online forums as an outlet for various frustrations, directing their anger and insults mostly towards the government (Frere 2014, 241).

While the incivility and unruliness of comments are common drawbacks of online readers' comments (see Chapter 5), journalists across the newsrooms also raised concerns about the hate speech and tribal slurs generated on comment threads. A senior reporter at *NewsDay* gave a detailed picture of these concerns:

> While it is important to be open-minded at all times, aberrant comments are such a distraction [...]. This is mostly the case in political stories where some readers drag in tribalism and it ends up a slinging match of 'tribalists' [...]. In such situations, the issues that are central to the story get lost [...]. Sadly, some comments are insults directed to the subject of the story or readers fighting among themselves.

The widespread use of pseudonyms on the comment forums was particularly described as contributing to the dumbing down of the quality of contributions online. As one reporter explained: 'Readers find it easy to smuggle [sic] tribal issues on matters that are far divorced from it [...] because they are under cover and difficult to identify'. Thus, while anonymity has its advantages in contexts where the dangers of being identified are real, such as in Zimbabwe, it equally 'lowers both the "intellectual level" of comments and user responsibility for them' by creating a 'disinhibition effect' that leads to 'a reduced sense of responsibility and less pressure to conform to societal norms' (Reich 2011, 104). (We discuss the normative threats posed by readers' comments in detail in Chapter 5.)

Comments moderation and porous 'gatekeeping' approaches

The above concerns were largely rooted in the moderation and 'gatekeeping' dilemmas faced by newsrooms in managing UGC on their websites. Although 'gatekeeping' in general has traditionally been the preserve of editors, inconsistencies in the moderation approaches deployed for readers' comments on the websites of both the state-controlled and private press in Zimbabwe pointed to challenges faced in applying traditional standards to the new 'cacophonous world of participatory journalism' (Singer et al. 2011, 4). While there were clear differences in the attitudes and approaches taken across news organisations, they all broadly deployed loose forms of content restriction or filtering. This somewhat casual approach, especially for the privately owned AMH, was broadly influenced by the news organisations' response to the pervasive culture of censorship in Zimbabwe, which they described as potentially damaging to their readers' loyalty as well as the pragmatic challenges of 'winnowing' the massive volumes of UGC. Embracing an *open deliberative culture* and UGC on their websites was therefore primarily a strategic posture. As AMH's group online editor explained: 'we have deliberately, wrongly or rightly, let people talk because we don't want to be associated with the well-known culture of censorship [...]. We want traffic to increase on our websites'.

However, despite this 'non-moderation' posture, all newsrooms claimed to be particularly vigilant with regard to incitements to hatred, abuse, crime or defamation on their websites, which resulted in forms of content restriction. As Zimpapers' group online editor explained:

> We're forced to censor for foul language and information which is not factual because it is easier to be sued when a comment appears on the website [...]. We censor some words that we feel are abusive and not good for a family newspaper. But I've got to admit, [...] sometimes the volume overwhelms us.

Online editors also claimed to keep a close eye on political content likely to trigger hostile responses from various centres of power. However, as already noted, there were divergences in the approaches taken by the two news organisations. While Zimpapers generally deployed an overt and firmer approach codified in a policy document articulating 'community rules and guidelines' for users posted on its newspapers websites,[2] AMH on the other hand took a more relaxed approach. These divergent approaches not only point to the fact that there is no silver bullet concerning what kind of moderation system is used across news organisations, but also echoes Deuze's (2003) view that news organisations tend to expand their operations to the Internet based on their existing journalistic culture, including the way they relate to the public. Explaining the reasoning behind the setting up of guidelines for readers, Zimpapers' group online editor stated: 'The policy is informed by our editorial thrust as well as the country's laws. People can sue us, so we ensure that as people comment on our stories, they know what's allowed and what isn't'. The setting up of terms and conditions for users should thus be seen in the broader context of Zimpapers' entrenched culture of 'innate conservatism' (Mabweazara 2013) as well as a deep-rooted reluctance to relinquish 'power' to readers as discussed earlier. Consequently, while there is a professed attempt to facilitate free expression on the readers' comments sections, there remains a reluctance to surrender the traditional gatekeeping role (Hermida 2011b).

On the other hand, the relaxed moderation approach adopted by the privately owned AMH was obvious in the lack of a codified 'gatekeeping' policy beyond an informal statement of appeal to readers to avoid posting 'profane, tribalistic, racist, libellous or malicious comments' displayed on all its newspaper websites.[3] It is for this reason that most journalists at AMH were not clear whether there was any moderation taking place. However, despite this lack of clarity and the posturing noted earlier, it was evident that there was some degree of control over content posted on the newspaper websites as noted above. Thus, within the inconsistent approaches to moderation, one notes a cocktail of intricately connected loose strategies of gatekeeping used by online editors across the newsroom, as shown in Figure 2.1.

Collectively, these approaches can be interpreted as limiting the potential for competing views as well as the free flow of alternative ideas since some voices are either silenced or totally banished from entering these 'invited' spaces of user participation. In addition, as noted earlier, the moderation strategies also highlight the 'undemocratic' and the *janus-faced* nature of online comment sections. While on the one hand, they allow for deliberation and news engagement, on the other, they allow news organisations to shape the conversations through deletion, hiding and blocking of undesirable content.

Across both Zimpapers and AMH, limited resources, including shortages of manpower, were noted as militating against maintaining foolproof control over their readers' comment forums. For example, at the time of conducting research for this study, Zimpapers' group online editor was singlehandedly responsible for managing content on the organisation's seven newspaper websites. Similarly, AMH's group online editor was responsible for overseeing content on four newspapers. This scenario reduced 'gatekeeping' to an ad hoc, porous and tokenistic approach akin to what Bruns (2008) refers to as 'gatewatching', mostly hinged on a postpublication moderation system, which taps into the 'wisdom of the crowd to decide which commenters should be heard and which should be muted' (Santana 2011, 78). This is primarily due to the overwhelming volume of comments as well as the general pressure to maintain website traffic in a context where newspaper readership is shrinking, as elsewhere across the globe (see Chapter 4 for a discussion of AI-driven content moderation, which some newsrooms are adopting and deploying as a way of circumnavigating the challenges and intensity of filtering huge volumes of UGC).

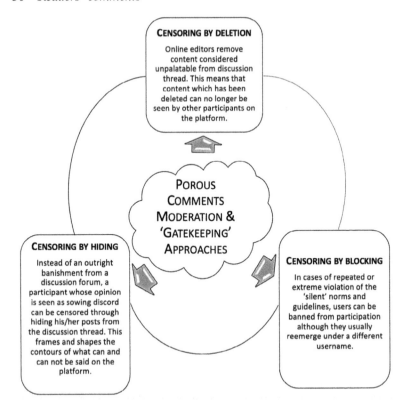

Figure 2.1 Loose strategies of moderating user comments used across news-rooms (adapted from Mare 2016, 222–223)

Conclusion

This chapter has examined how some newsrooms are adapting to the 'participatory culture' associated with readers' comments on newspaper websites as well as the challenges and professional implications emerging with this new 'media ecology'. In general, the study demonstrates that although the newsrooms are still largely adjusting to the practice of interactivity and the permeation of readers' voices into their territory, the developments are influencing and challenging newsroom practices in ways that point to an ecological reconfiguration of the established news culture. Readers' comments are providing a useful extra layer of functionality that complements existing practices through providing story ideas, engendering public debate as well as 'holding journalists to account' by exposing poor journalistic practice and ethical transgressions. In the same way, the lack of effective gatekeeping strategies has opened floodgates to abusive and extremist comments that pose serious threats to the core values and normative ideals of traditional journalism (see Chapter 5). The study's findings broadly point to divergent and ad hoc approaches to the gatekeeping of comments sections across the state-controlled and the private press, a scenario that broadly mirrors related experiences in the Global North. Whereas Zimpapers generally deploys an overt and firmer approach codified in policy, AMH takes a laissez-faire approach. As elsewhere on the African continent, these divergent approaches affirm the news organisations' expansion to the web based on their prevailing journalistic culture, including the way they relate to their audiences. In a polarised media environment, these approaches also mirror the broader socio-political landscape where because of the existing political economy and the authoritarian stances of the ruling party, the state-controlled press is generally expected to follow a stricter culture of filtering and censorship, whereas the private media tends to uphold a relaxed approach to gatekeeping consonant with democratic values.

Across all newsrooms studied, however, it is clear that the incivility and unruliness of readers' comments are a key challenge. The proliferation of hate speech and tribal slurs generated on comment threads is dumbing down discourses and deliberations. This requires a more clearly organised approach, beyond simply tapping into the 'wisdom of the crowd' (Santana 2011, 78) in order to raise the level of discourse. Overall, there is still far more to discover in this area. Numerous questions remain about how readers participate in the news process, as well as what we can glean from a close examination of the discourses churned out on the comment forums beyond simply looking at what the journalists say they do with the comments, as this chapter has broadly attempted to do.

Notes

1 AMH's group editor-in-chief, Vincent Kahiya, speaking at the launch of a new edition, the *Southern Eye*, by the group. Retrieved from: www.southerneye.co. zw/2013/05/31/ncube-speaks-on-southern-eye-launch/ [accessed 3 June 2019].
2 See Zimbabwe Newspapers (1980) Limited Website Terms and Conditions. Retrieved from: www.herald.co.zw/copyright/ [accessed 20 June 2020].
3 See 'Important Notice to our readers'. Retrieved from: www.newsday.co.zw/ 2013/06/24/important-notice-to-our-readers/ [accessed 3 June, 2014].

3 The social media turn and news engagement

In general, social media platforms have been implicated in the disruption of institutionalised newsrooms, spawning what some scholars have called the 'decentred newsroom' (Mare 2014) in which news content can be generated and filed from anywhere but the newsroom itself, thanks to smartphones and a reliable Internet connection. In many ways, social media platforms have significantly transformed the 'landscape of newsgathering [as well as] the resulting journalistic products, relationships, routines, and culture' (Robinson 2011, 1123). Extending this view further, Broersma and Eldridge II (2019, 193) postulate that the emergence of social media platforms and 'their adoption by news media and other social actors have brought about a series of changes which have had an impact on how news is produced, how information is shared, how audiences consume news, and how publics are formed'. Platforms like WhatsApp groups, Facebook pages and Twitter hashtags have reconfigured the constitution of publics and opened up pathways for news sharing and viral distribution of content.

Several scholars concur that the technological affordances of social media such as peer production, interactive dialogue, collaboration, social connections and virality have reconfigured traditional journalism from largely a *monologue* into a *dialogical* social activity (Bruns & Highfield 2012; Meikle & Young 2012). Despite the initial unease with embracing these platforms in the newsroom, it is important to highlight 'the gradual but inexorable influence of social media logics on professional journalism' (Bruns & Nuernbergk 2019, 206), especially through the emergence of what Pavlik frames as a 'two-way symmetric model of communication' in which the flow of communication is 'much more a dialog between both or all parties to communication' (2000, 235–236). This development is credited for 'shifting power around' and 'reflecting a deep urge among citizens for a more direct and open form of [...] communication' (Beckett 2008, 126). As a result, 'the ways journalism and social media have intertwined have become more complex as actors at all levels – from the subjects of coverage, to journalists, to those consuming news – engage [simultaneously] within these spaces' (Broersma & Eldridge II 2019, 193).

Platforms like Facebook, Twitter, YouTube and WhatsApp have allowed the erstwhile passive consumers to participate in news production, distribution and engagement activities through citizen journalism (Moyo D. 2009). These social media platforms have not only resulted in an increasingly 'active audience' but also recalibrated the way people receive and share information, including how journalists interact with news sources (Mabweazara 2014). Routine practices like posting comments and sharing news through Facebook, WhatsApp and Twitter have become significant news consumption rituals. This has allowed news to migrate from one platform to another in ways that complicate news engagement in the broader communicative ecology, which has become a hybrid space where various actors engage with each other in different ways that are establishing new power structures.

Similarly, however, as more journalists across socio-economic divides discover the relevance of the interactive platforms in their lives and work, platforms like WhatsApp and Facebook are also being berated for limiting conversations to a 'self-selecting' elite social group as well as facilitating the spread of fake news, misinformation and disinformation (see Chapter 4 and 5). In this chapter, we explore the complex intersections between a range of social media platforms and emerging user participatory cultures that are shaping and redefining news production and consumption practices.

The 'architecture' of popular social media platforms in African journalism

For our purposes in this book, the term *social media* is used interchangeably with *Web 2.0 technologies*. As Fuchs (2017, 34) observes, both terms have in the past years become popular for describing types of World Wide Web (www) applications, such as blogs, microblogs like Twitter, social network sites like Facebook, video, image and file sharing platforms, wikis or mobile instant messaging applications like WhatsApp and WeChat. According to O'Reilly (2005), Web 2.0 applications are those that make the most of the intrinsic advantages of that platform: delivering software as a continually updated service that gets better the more people use it, consuming and remixing data from multiple sources, including individual users, while providing their own data and services in a form that allows remixing by others. All this creates network effects through an 'architecture of participation' that delivers rich user experiences. This *architecture of participation* and *interactivity* has been hailed by techno-optimists as responsible for laying a solid foundation for the growth and continuous evolution of 'participatory journalism' (Singer et al. 2011, see Chapter 1). Social media platforms allow audiences to comment, share, like, retweet and even send private messages to media organisations and journalists rather than engage in the passive consumption of news.

van Dijck (2013, 11) argues that the word '*social*' in social media also implies that platforms are user-centred. It is also believed that they facilitate communal activities by 'allowing people to collaborate, play, share, and communicate' (boyd 2009). Thus, interactivity and audience participation are some of the standout communal activities associated with the 'social media turn'. In line with Jenkins' (2006) theory of convergence culture, social media platforms are seen as contributing significantly to the 'blurring of the distinction between personal communication (to be shared one-to-one) and public media (to be shared with nobody in particular)' (Meikle & Young 2012, 68). As discussed above, social media have also been accompanied by the conflation between *production* and *consumption*, which has been theorised by Bruns (2008) as bringing into existence the phenomenon of 'produsage'. This concept acknowledges the blurring of the boundaries between passive consumption and active production.

Some of the social media platforms that have gained traction in the context of African journalism are summarised in Figure 3.1.

While the above categorisation is useful, it is important to highlight that the boundaries between the different types of social media are becoming increasingly blurred. For example, Shi et al. (2014) argue that Twitter is a combination of broadcasting service and social network and classify it as a 'social broadcasting technology'. Equally worth acknowledging is the fact that '[n]ew media and new apps are continually appearing which offer new functionality or combine the various types of social media in new ways' (McKenna et al. 2017, 89).

A key feature of the above social media platforms which accounts for their popularity and close connection with *context-specific participatory practices* in Africa (as discussed in Chapter 1) is the notion of 'virality', 'an allegory of rapid distribution of information and ideas' (Denisova 2020, 1), which according to Alhabash and McAlister, 'reflects the sophistication of interactivity on social media' (2015, 1318). In their tripartite overview of virality, they submit that it emphasises users' behaviours in relation to:

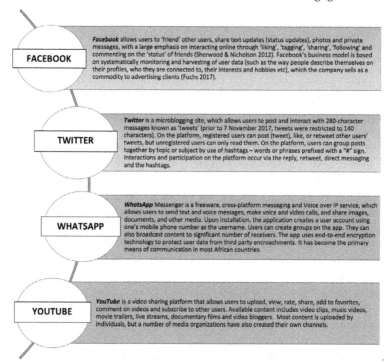

Figure 3.1 Popular social media platforms in African newsrooms

1   *Viral reach*, which 'refers to the volume of message sharing and forwarding by [social media] users. It indicates the number of users that have proactively shared and forwarded a message with their online and/or offline social networks' (Alhabash & McAlister 2015, 1318–1319). This can also be seen as the 'electronic word-of-mouth' (p. 1318).

2   *Affective evaluation*, in which 'social media users express their affective responses to online messages in ways that are visible to others'. For example, users can 'like', 'love', or express anger at a Facebook message (p. 1319).

3   *Message deliberation*, which 'deals with Internet users' active and public deliberation of online messages' (p. 1319).

Social media *virality* closely relates to popular grassroots communication practices and channels such as 'pavement sidewalk radio', cartoons, memes, jokes and subvertisements, which collectively constitute informal and unofficial platforms used by African citizens to engage and deliberate on critical current affairs. These forms of popular communication tend to circulate and spread widely online via social media, SMS, and offline, via word of mouth, thus constituting sites for context-specific forms of participatory journalism. On these sites, news stories and current affairs are 'amplified, sustained and potentially morphed as they are re-circulated, reworked, and reframed by online networks' (Goode 2009, 1293) (we return to these participatory practices in detail later in this chapter).

Overall, the architecture of social media platforms simultaneously enables and restricts particular modes of participation and interaction. This is partly because they are influenced by a specific programming code (Mare 2016). This observation chimes with MacKenzie and Wajcman's (1999) view that technologies can be designed, consciously or unconsciously, to open certain social options and close others. For the purposes of this chapter, we rely on illustrative examples from Facebook, Twitter, YouTube and WhatsApp.

It is important to highlight that asymmetries in Internet access continue to manifest along class, geography (mostly an urban phenomenon), gender and race lines in most African countries (Mare 2016). This is partly due to high costs of broadband Internet, lack of electricity, dilapidated telecommunications infrastructure and other structural impediments. For these reasons, the penetration rate of social media platforms in Africa has not yet reached the proportions present in the Global North (Mare 2016). Although disaggregated data on the penetration rates of platforms like WhatsApp, Twitter and YouTube in Africa is extremely hard to find, periodic country reports released by the telecommunications regulatory authorities have consistently revealed that these sites are very popular, especially among young people.

In the light of the above, our empirical research in selected African countries shows that beyond the generic technological affordances of social media, which have broadened audience participation, localised appropriations of the platforms have resulted in *context-specific participatory practices and cultures* that collectively point to the 'social shaping' nature of technology (Bijker 1995). The creative deployment of the platforms by media organisations, individual journalists and audiences further emphasises the idea that technologies have 'interpretive flexibility' as opposed to a rigid and 'linear' applicability advocated for by technological determinists.

Social media and participatory journalism

A sizeable body of literature examining the relationship between social media and participatory journalism has emerged in the past decade. Most of this research is dominated by Western scholarship which sees *social media as a boon*, resulting in more access, more interactivity, and the possibility of embedding news and conversations about it in social networks (see Hermida 2010; Gulyas 2013; Kammer 2013; Broersma & Eldridge II 2019). For these scholars, the platforms have opened up interactive and participatory channels which are instrumental for news organisations to revitalise relationships with their 'imagined audiences' as discussed in the preceding chapter. Drawing on the participatory affordances of these platforms, Jenkins (2006) has theorised about the rise of a 'participatory media culture' while Mandiberg talks of the liberation of audiences from the elite-centric news agenda and 'the unbridled outflow of user-generated content (UGC)' (2012, 2). Jenkins' (2006) participatory media culture refers to a culture with relatively low barriers to civic engagement, strong support for making and sharing creations, and some type of informal mentorship in which experienced participants pass along knowledge to novices. Far from being passive recipients of media content from professional journalists, these empowered audiences are 'employing press [and broadcast] tools they have in their possession to inform one another' (Rosen 2006).

Only a handful of studies conducted in the African context have focused on how media organisations have appropriated social media platforms, primarily Facebook and Twitter, for newsgathering, distribution and audience participation purposes. Writing from the Mozambican context, Mare (2014) for example, investigates how a small community newspaper in Maputo, @*Verdade*, has embraced social media platforms in its news production and engagement drive. Similarly, Mabweazara (2014) examines how Zimbabwean print newsrooms have adjusted themselves in the light of participatory affordances of social media platforms. He observes that the 'viral connections' engendered by social media platforms have facilitated a rise in UGC. This permeation of UGC into the news media ecology hitherto dominated by professionally generated content has challenged the traditional definition of journalism and the intricate interaction between the 'power of the media producer and the power of the media consumer' (Jenkins 2006, 2). It has not only disrupted news production and consumption but also transmogrified gatekeeping and audience participation practices and cultures across the world. As social media platforms gained societal traction across the globe, media organisations and journalists have been quick to establish accounts, realising the potential benefits of directly engaging with their audience, promoting their brands, distributing their content and forging strategic relationships with news sources (Mare 2014).

More importantly, the interactivity fostered by social media has reconfigured the relationships between news organisations and their publics (Mudhai 2014). The 'new normal' on social media is also characterised by the hybrid mixing of private contexts and professional practices as boundaries between personal and professional, public and private spaces collapse and intermesh (Mabweazara 2013). It has enabled journalists to move closer to engaging with their audiences in hitherto unseen ways (Mudhai 2011; Paterson 2013). The chasm, which existed between journalists (as producers/senders) and audiences (as consumers/receivers) in the classical audience theorisation of mass communication has blurred. Similarly, the ability to engage with news and with other news consumers is giving readers greater influence over the material covered in news media while at the same time providing journalists with an opportunity to access ideas and leads from the readers (Moyo, D. 2009).

Because of the underlying logic of 'openness and participation' (Lewis 2012, 840) associated with social media, traditional editorial 'gatekeeping' structures in the newsmaking processes have been thrown up in the air as 'authority is dispersed and shared' (Gulyas 2013, 272) among platform companies, professionals and ordinary citizens. An increase in the platform companies and audience's 'power' is seen as accompanied by the waning of journalists' gatekeeping and agenda-setting influences (Singer et al. 2011). As Broersma and Eldridge II (2019) surmise, the shifting away from a situation where the news agenda is wholly controlled by news organisations and journalists towards social media where control is partly surrendered to large platform companies can be described as the 'dislocation of news'. It points to fundamental changes in the way news is presented as well as to shifts in 'power redistribution from the *news media* to *platform companies*' (Westlund & Ekström 2018, 5, emphasis original). The practices also speak to the emerging dependencies between the news media and social media companies, although the former relies heavily on the latter for distributing their content and engaging with audiences.

As elsewhere, these changes are not without normative dilemmas for African news organisations (see discussion in Chapter 5). As with readers' comments discussed in the preceding chapter, 'dark forms of participation' (Quandt 2018) on social media platforms appropriated by news organisations have undermined the credibility of readers' comments and engagements. This has further been worsened by the explosion of 'fake news', disinformation and cyber-propaganda on social media platforms (see Mare et al. 2019). Moreover, dependence on social media content is also turning some journalists into 'data consumers' as opposed to being 'creators' (Peters 2011, 155). Peters further warns that 'news organisations that become too integrated with social media risk losing the very things that made them vital' (p. 159), that is, sourcing and verifying news in situ outside interactive digital platforms. As with the comments sections on newspaper websites, these normative dilemmas are exacerbated by moderation challenges on social media platforms (see Chapters 2 and 5).

Crowdsourcing, audience participation and news engagement

One of the main findings of this study is that the widespread use of social media in professional journalistic contexts and society in general is offering African citizens a broader spectrum of opportunities to engage in 'participatory journalism' as defined in Chapter 1. Platforms like Facebook, WhatsApp and Twitter are offering citizens across sub-Saharan Africa opportunities to engage directly with mainstream news as readers and contributors to news content. Our research revealed that social media platforms have been incorporated into journalistic processes across newsrooms for a myriad of reasons, including: to uncover and gather news tips; pursue and cultivate news sources; reach out and connect with news sources; follow influential newsmakers (politicians, businesspeople, celebrities, social media influencers etc.); gauge the public mood on topical social issues and current affairs; report and clarify rumours, gossip and 'fake news'; and to promote news content and interact with a broad section of audiences. Social media platforms have thus stretched journalism's sourcing strategies by opening up its news *procurement black boxes* to the 'people formerly known as the audience' (Rosen 2006).

A key element of this extension of the sourcing strategies to include ordinary citizens is the reinvigoration of the *wisdom of the crowd* (as well as the *ignorance of the crowd*) which has given rise to what Aitamurto (2016) calls 'crowdsourced journalism' in African journalism. This form of journalism is made possible by the technological affordances of social media, especially its 'spreadability' (Jenkins 2006) or 'viral reach' (Alhabash & McAlister 2015; Denisova 2020). In *crowdsourcing*, 'the journalist treats crowd input as raw material and weaves it into the story in the ways that she or he thinks is appropriate, but – it is the journalist who writes the story' (Aitamurto 2016, 186). As an emerging sourcing strategy, crowdsourcing is seen as a model for distributing reporting across many people (i.e. the crowd). It constitutes the bridge through which a news organisation broadens its 'procurement channels' through the careful integration of the crowd (the public) as a news supplier. A good example of this is shown in Figure 3.2, which shows the Managing Editor of Uganda's *Daily Monitor* crowdsourcing ideas on Facebook on what questions to ask a prominent retired Army General and HIV/ AIDS activist ahead of a meeting with him. He reverts back to the same platform to engage the readers after doing the story.

Similar crowdsourcing examples can be seen elsewhere across newsrooms in Southern Africa. A number of interviews with journalists revealed that because most of their news sources and readers have a strong presence on social media platforms like Facebook, Twitter and WhatsApp, it has become cheaper for them to crowdsource news stories on these sites rather than practice 'traditional shoe-leather reporting' (Mabweazara 2013), which involves chasing after and engaging with news sources in situ, within their 'natural settings' or through their often unanswered phones. As one senior reporter at the privately owned *NewsDay* newspaper in Zimbabwe put it: 'Social networking sites have become a one-stop shop for all kinds of journalists'. The importance of lurking in platforms like WhatsApp groups in order to identify newsworthy ideas was also noted by another journalist at *The*

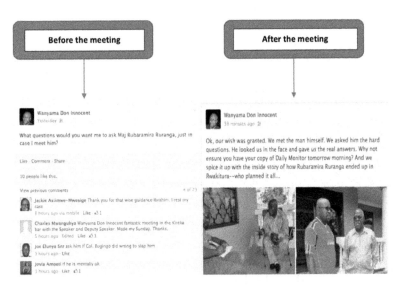

Figure 3.2 The Managing Editor of Uganda's *Daily Monitor* crowdsourcing ideas and engaging readers on a story generated on Facebook

Herald in Zimbabwe: 'I subscribe into some WhatsApp [groups and] in those groups, I'm often a silent observer, following and monitoring rumours, which I then verify with authoritative sources'.

These experiences in Zimbabwe were also corroborated by journalists elsewhere on the continent. In response to questions on the impact of social media on journalism, the Editor of *Confidante* in Namibia stated, '[social media] has made it possible for us to conduct opinion polls on very controversial issues like the #HandsOffHage and #BoycottIndependenceCelebrations. We occasionally browse news feeds and read comments for possible story ideas'. This use of social media to crowd source story ideas, comments and general insights from sources scattered across the globe, consequently supplementing or even supplanting their traditional news sourcing strategies, is acknowledged by a number of scholars (see Mabweazara 2013; Aitamurto 2016). It also demonstrates that journalism has become an *'open black box'* where journalists and their audience are engaged in an ongoing collaborative work.

Some journalists suggested that before pitching stories during their traditional early morning diary meetings they usually post probing questions to their inquisitive audiences and followers on social media for news tips and ideas. Others reported that they go through the social media comment sections of their previous stories to get a sense of developing stories or ideas for follow-up stories. A classic example of this is related to radio current affairs talk show hosts who deploy social media to crowd-source questions they intend to field to panellists on their programmes. This practice is particularly evident during live streams on YouTube and Facebook as well as live phone-in programmes. As Figure 3.3 shows, in addition to allowing audiences to contribute to programmes using social media comments sections, some media organisations use the platforms to share their studio phone numbers, WhatsApp contact details and Twitter handles of programme hosts.

Media organisations in Kenya, Zimbabwe, Namibia and South Africa are no longer relying exclusively on the traditional letters-to-the-editor but have embraced multiple platforms, including SMS, emails and WhatsApp, through which solicited news engagement takes place as shown above. In Namibia, *The Namibian* charges N$1 (which is equivalent to about US$0.05) for each SMS sent by their readers as part of the letters-to-the-editor (code named 'What You're Saying'). This points to attempts by the newspaper to commercialise the letters-to-the-editor section in order to diversify its revenue income streams. Similarly, in another innovative effort to attract content from readers, some news organisations reward those who respond to social media calls to contribute journalistic content. For example, *H-Metro*, a

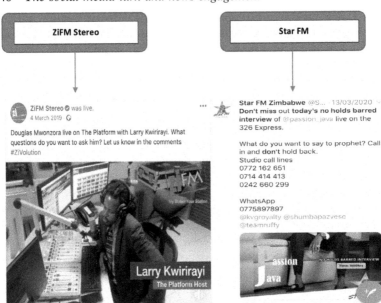

Figure 3.3 ZiFM Stereo and Star FM radio stations in Zimbabwe calling on their listeners to submit questions for their panellists on Facebook and Twitter

tabloid newspaper in Zimbabwe, pays citizen journalists for capturing pictures, which are published on their 'social scene' page (Mare 2014). However, most media organisations in Africa rely on voluntary netizens to update them on real time news events happening within their local settings. As Brabham (2012) points out, the 'social media crowd' participates in voluntary crowdsourcing because of intrinsically driven motivations, such as a sense of civic duty to contribute, ideological reasoning, or the fun derived from the activity.

In addition to the above participatory practices, readers *engage with* and *influence* mainstream news on social media platforms by commenting, evaluating and sharing with other social media users. As shown in Figure 3.4, readers extract news nuggets from newspapers by taking photographs or screenshots and commenting or evaluating before sharing. The extracted news nuggets and additional commentary circulate via a complex intermeshing ecosystem of platforms and social spaces that include Twitter, Facebook and WhatsApp Groups, as well as via SMS or 'pavement radio' for those with poor Internet connectivity (we return to the latter point shortly). Because journalists and

Figure 3.4 A reader comments on and shares mainstream news nuggets on Twitter

other primary news definers or agenda setters are part of these networks, this form of news engagement inadvertently leads to forms of 'reciprocity [or] relational exchange between professional journalists and audiences/amateur news participants' (Wall 2017, 135) in ways that influence or shape newsmaking. This reinforces Oeldorf-Hirsch's (2018, 226) view that 'although news consumption [and sharing] on social media is more incidental than through traditional media, it offers [readers] more opportunities to engage with news content' by discussing, commenting and sharing their views with a wider community that includes journalists.

Print media and the intricacies of participation and news engagement

While ordinary citizens are indeed influencing and shaping print media content, it is important to note that 'the power [still] lies within the journalist who decides when, where, and how crowdsourcing happens. The journalist also decides how the crowd's input is used' (Aitamurto 2016, 186). This kind of *managed participation* (Willems 2013) on social media reproduces intricate power imbalances between platform companies, journalists and the audience. Furthermore, in social contexts where the digital divide is more pronounced, crowdsourcing journalism has the unintended consequences of promoting elite-centric news sourcing approaches, where social media influencers, politicians and celebrities dominate the *news agenda setting equation* (see Chapter 5). In other words, *choreographed participation* via social media does not radically democratise the newsmaking agenda but allows media organisations and journalists to cherry pick news ideas, which advance their editorial policies. This also dovetails with earlier studies which indicate that users are typically offered only a low level of influence through generic technological affordances that enable them to react to news articles by, among other things, commenting on social media pages (see Hermida & Thurman 2008). It often turns 'out to be little more than "marketing", programmed just to fill gaps in broadcasting schedules or to increase audience ratings' (Carpentier et al., 2019, 19).

For most print media organisations in Africa, participation can be defined as either *solicited* or *unsolicited* (Willems 2013). In solicited participation, media organisations encourage their audience to participate, whether by phone, social media or their websites (Willems 2013). In the latter, the audience take the initiative to spontaneously engage with news content through various platforms, including the social media pages of news organisations. While this kind of participation or projection of 'voice' through texting or leaving a comment on social media has now become the 'new normal', it is important to highlight that in the context of 'surveillance capitalism' (Zuboff 2019), the audience are parting with their personal data and income, which eventually contributes to a healthier revenue base for media organisations (Willems 2013).

Solicited news engagement can also take the format of opinion polls, asking open-ended questions and direct seeking of feedback from the audience. Newspapers like the *NewsDay* (Zimbabwe), the *Mail & Guardian* (South Africa) and *The Namibian* (Namibia) have also experimented with online polls as a way of cajoling their readers into engaging with their social media platforms. This represents another *innovative* albeit *elitist* way of conducting opinion polls on serious national issues. Although most of the polls posted on social media did not elicit a lot of online engagement (at least via *likes, comments, shares* and *replies*), it is arguable that such invited spaces of participation have fostered what Hermida (2010, 301) calls 'ambient journalism' – information networks that provide an 'asynchronous, lightweight and always-on communication system [...] enabling citizens to maintain a mental model of news and events around them'.

Beyond harnessing the participatory affordances of technology, the appropriation of social media platforms has been intricately enmeshed with local conditions of access, affordability and contextual adaptability. Newspapers are adopting and adapting social media participatory experiences and affordances to offline situations. For example, community newspapers like Mozambique's *@Verdade*, have recreated a physical 'Facebook wall' on a perimeter durawall surrounding their premises (see Figure 3.5). On this physical 'Facebook wall', citizens can post news tips, complaints on service delivery challenges and act as whistle blowers on corruption cases. The recreation of an online 'Facebook wall' in the physical space thus enables ordinary citizens to articulate issues of critical importance to their community in graphic formats and other UGC forms, which demonstrates that African newsrooms are drawing upon their socio-technological and cultural resources to develop genres that meet their needs and expectations (Bijker 1995; Mare 2014).

The 'physical Facebook wall' therefore articulates the local specificities of participatory journalism in resource-constrained contexts.

Figure 3.5 News tips, comments and complaints on *@Verdade*'s physical 'Facebook wall' outside the newspaper's offices in Maputo, Mozambique (photo credit: Admire Mare)

Thus, rather than relying on the virtual sphere, ordinary citizens are feeding into 'crowdsourced journalism' through posting their story ideas on a physical wall. This provides an offline platform for the audience to interrogate topical issues in Maputo. Similar to online comments on social media, offline avenues like the 'physical wall' are enabling readers to contribute to a reconfigured news media ecology that is increasingly becoming more *dialogue-based* than *one-way*. These offline comments provide additional detail and insight to articles from informed readers who are passionate about the subject. They offer a wide range of supplementary opinions and give newsrooms a window into how their readers see both their journalism and the world around them. The feedback and perspectives can also broaden the publication's news coverage, inspire new stories and provide possible sources or ways to address an issue.

In line with the overarching argument of this book, the innovative creation by journalists at @*Verdade* further demonstrates that participatory journalism is 'socially constructed by situated actors working in a given social context' (Orlikowski 1992, 406). In a context where the digital inequalities and questions of access are the order of the day as is the case in most sub-Saharan African countries, the *physical Facebook wall* allows those who are still unconnected to participate in the newsmaking agenda, albeit in ways that are set by the designers of the 'platform' (the @*Verdade* editorial team in this case).

The appropriations of social media in the routine practices of newsrooms in Africa was further demonstrated by the localised integration of social media content into the institutionalised bureaucratic daily routines through which 'gate-keeping' decisions are rendered in the newsmaking processes, particularly through 'diary' and 'conference' meetings. At @*Verdade*, newsworthy content drawn from Facebook and Twitter is manually reproduced on the newsroom's noticeboard with sticky notes used to update and capture the most topical issues as they emerge on the platforms (see Figure 3.6). This encourages journalists to openly engage with the content by picking each other's brains, commenting on the relevance of what others have posted and collectively integrating the content into the formal editorial decision-making processes. Alongside the recreation of the online 'Facebook wall', this practice not only points to localised creative adaptations but also highlights how new technologies acquire new meanings in the complexities of the social contexts in which technologies are appropriated. The practice also points to the fact that social media involves different levels of engagement that extend online interactions to offline engagements.

Figure 3.6 @*Verdade's* noticeboard replicating what happens on Twitter and Facebook (photo credit: Admire Mare)

Broadcast media, audience news consumption and engagement

African broadcast news organisations have not been left out of the 'participatory journalism' bandwagon – a trend that sits within 'global transformations in the [broadcast] media sector' (Srinivasan & Diepeveen 2018, 390) thanks to the proliferation of digital communication technologies. Following the footsteps of international media organisations operating in Africa such as the British Broadcasting Corporation (BBC) World Service, Aljazeera, Cable News Network (CNN) and China Global Television Network (CGTN), commercial and public service broadcasters have adopted various social media channels to enhance their news production routines and audience engagements efforts. In addition to the traditional avenues of audience participation (such as inviting viewers to send an SMS or to email their messages), African television stations have set up social media accounts where both solicited and unsolicited forms of news engagement occur. The South African Broadcasting Corporation (SABC), Namibia Broadcasting Corporation (NBC) and Zimbabwe Broadcasting Corporation (ZBC), are among some of the state-controlled public broadcasters that are creatively appropriating social media platforms to build a close relationship with their audience.

The connections with audiences have largely been made possible by the widely acknowledged rapid rise in the use of 'mobile telephony, and its convergence with [traditional] broadcast media' since the early 2000s across Africa (Srinivasan & Diepeveen 2018, 395). It is for this reason that the mobile phone has occupied a central position in discourses about participatory journalism in Africa (see Moyo, D. 2009; Paterson 2013). Mobile-friendly popular social media platforms like Facebook and YouTube are facilitating new interactive broadcast formats that enable audience participation and offer completely new experiences in news consumption and engagement. Broadcasters are delivering live and pre-packaged news content to an audience located far and wide, beyond their 'homeland'.

These new transmission possibilities present 'a clear evolution' in African television broadcasting, which is now characterised by 'different and expansive possibilities for audience participation' (Srinivasan & Diepeveen 2018, 395). As Figure 3.7 shows, the interactive

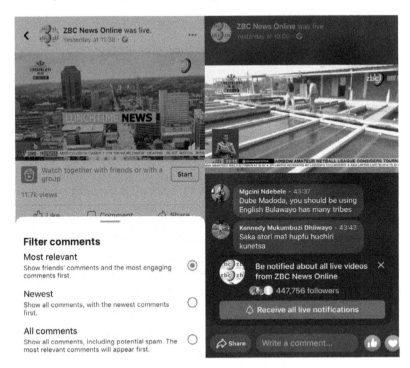

Figure 3.7 Zimbabwe Broadcasting Corporation's (ZBC) Interactive (Live) News Broadcast on Facebook

broadcasts on Facebook offer audiences distinct spaces for discussion, commenting and general engagement with the news content. Audiences can watch with friends or with a group, they can filter the comments for the most relevant and engaging ones or simply go through all the comments and 'express their affective responses' through 'likes', 'loves', etc. in ways that are visible to others (Alhabash & McAlister 2015, 1318). All this can take place in real time (at the moment of the live broadcasts) or way after the live broadcast.

From this, we can also surmise, as do Srinivasan and Diepeveen (2018, 390), that engaged and digitally connected audiences 'are actively involved in giving meaning' to news content on the interactive digital platforms 'in a shared "public" dialogue and, therefore, [...] involved in production' or at least in the shaping of coverage and 'information flows' in some ways (see also Paterson 2013). It is also important to highlight that, beyond providing audiences with an opportunity to watch news as well as connect at a local and global scale, the engagements and connections take place by means of a 'localisation' and 'domestication' of the digital technologies which, in the case of interactions captured in Figure 3.7, are heavily shaped by local politics and the use of local languages.

Several broadcasters have also set up WhatsApp accounts for news tips and feedback from their audience (see Figure 3.3 for examples from radio stations in Zimbabwe). On SABC's current affairs programmes such as *Morning Live, Newsroom, Full View* and *Network*, viewers across the African continent and beyond are invited to send their input via text messages, audio, video and images. Equally, most of SABC's international news channel programmes have a 'Question of the Day' slot where audiences are encouraged to respond via Twitter, Facebook, WhatsApp voice notes and SMS. These technologies are also distinctly reshaping the possibilities of broadcast journalism in Namibia, where the NBC has been a torchbearer in embracing interactive social media platforms during news bulletins. For example, during NBC's News at 8, the public broadcaster dedicates a substantial amount of time to reading out selected comments from their social media platforms.

The popularity of interactive broadcast news programmes and the active participation of audiences on platforms as seen above indicate a perceived value by African audiences. There is no denying that the technological affordances of social media platforms have played a key role in evoking audiences' interests and in shaping the nature of news engagement and participation. As Willems and Mano (2016) suggest, digital media have afforded African audiences the opportunity to move beyond the largely passive audience experiences of legacy media to being active users of digital media, often in combination with older forms of media. However, as noted earlier, the architecture of participation remains constrained by the design features and generic technological affordances of interactive platforms as well as questions of access.

Likewise, the new opportunities for participation and news engagement should not only be seen as shaped and influenced by socio-technical features, nor should the popularity of technological affordances be seen as suggesting that African audiences have not traditionally engaged directly with news media, including broadcast news and current affairs. As Willems (2013) aptly argues, African audience participation in content production precedes newer communication technologies, as evident in letter writing, phone-in programmes and other locally contingent communicative avenues as we discuss below.

Context-specific forms of 'participatory journalism' in Africa

The African communicative ecology has always been characterised by elements of *participatory journalism* associated with newer technologies such as social media. These include notions such as '*sharing, collaboration*, and opportunities for users to both *create* their own material' (Meikle 2016, 4, emphasis added) and to *circulate* it in established *social networks*.[1] Consequently, popular forms of communication in Africa are inherently characterised by *communal* and *collaborative* practices that allow ordinary people to produce, edit, repurpose and remix information, news, images, artwork and videos into their own unique creations that deliver rich, 'spreadable' user experiences. It is in this light that Goode (2009) reminds us that journalism in Africa has always existed alongside a range of other unique forms of 'localised' news dissemination, communication and storytelling practices. This observation, as we attempt to show in this section, reinforces the need to think beyond scholarly accounts that restrict our understanding of *participatory journalism* to 'generic technological affordances'. Thus, while there is no question that *participatory journalism* is broadly sustained by technological affordances as seen in the better part of this book, it is equally important to acknowledge that interactive digital technologies are intimately bound up with local socio-political, economic and cultural circumstances which shape and constrain how they are deployed in specific contexts (see Bijker 1995; Barney et al. 2016). As Wasserman aptly contends, rather than adopt a purely deterministic approach, we need to 'view technology and society in interaction' (2011, 156) or as a 'duality of influences' (Mare 2014). This approach enables us to look at Africa, in its complex and diverse nature, as an 'epistemological location' that is 'grounded in particular contexts, worldviews and knowledge systems' (Willems & Mano 2016, 4–5) that collectively shape communication practices, including *participatory journalism*.

Against this backdrop, this section attempts to show the unique forms of participatory journalism in Africa as well as broadly argue that African citizens have always creatively used locally available channels of communication (and resources) to engage, play, share, communicate, contest and sometimes influence mainstream news and official sources of information (Nyamnjoh 2005).

Extending (participatory) journalism beyond traditional journalism

Prior to the popularisation of the concept of 'participatory journalism' in the Global North, scholars like Ellis (1989) had already begun theorising about the existence of 'pavement radio' (*radio trottoir*) in Africa, which as discussed in Chapter 1 refers to 'the popular and unofficial discussion of current affairs […], particularly in urban areas' (Ellis 1989, 321). Similarly, popular communication channels like memes, jokes, gossip, rumours, cartoons, music, art, graffiti, subvertisements and anonymous letters have always rivalled 'mainstream journalism in the ways [they address and engage with] political, social and economic realities' (Mano 2007, 61). These localised communicative practices, as Mano further submits, are an important part of the journalistic ecosystem, especially 'in contexts where public communication spaces are constrained, [and] censorship is high or where political communication is monopolised by a few people' (2007, 62), which is predominantly the case in most sub-Saharan African countries (see Mabweazara 2018).

In the 'social media era', communicative practices have become more prominent as more people actively bypass traditional information flows to experience media content via recommendations, shared links, WhatsApp groups, Twitter or Facebook (Paterson 2013). Thus, the creative use of social media has not only facilitated the digitisation of localised forms of popular communication such as 'pavement radio', but also led to the amplification of the voices of ordinary citizens who often struggle to get their voices into the mainstream public sphere or are constrained by censorship (Mano 2007; Moyo, D. 2009). Social media is also transforming the consumption of media content from a predominantly individualised experience into a communal activity in which audiences engage with the content as well as with each other on the same content in a complex and evolving form of news engagement.

As discussed earlier, the intrinsic affordances of social media also allow audiences to remix videos and audios, photoshop images, subvertise slogans and logos, and memify topical news and current affairs drawn from multiple sources, thus creating 'network effects' that deliver rich user experiences (O'Reilly 2005). Also, because of the relatively low barriers to artistic expression associated with Web 2.0 applications or social media in general, African citizens are increasingly engaging with mainstream news via 'a wide and ever-expanding array of genres' (Postema & Deuze 2020, 1308), which range from cartoons, through jokes, memes and subvertisements to photoshopped images. Thus, a broader definition of news that looks beyond the 'limited newsroom conceptions' (p. 1308) to include hitherto peripheral genres that engage with current affairs offers a more perceptive conception of 'participatory journalism' in Africa.

Taking this approach, Mano cites Zelizer to advocate 'seeing journalism through the lens of culture in order to expand its boundaries' to 'include outliers such as political cartoonists, tabloid hacks, political satirists, photojournalists and bloggers' (2007, 62) whose journalistic nature is collectively rooted in the way they capture contemporary 'social reality in its themes and content' as well as how they set 'the agenda for society' and for what mainstream journalists write about (Mano 2007, 62). Thus, a personal post on Twitter involving the use of emojis by the UK ambassador to Zimbabwe in the context of a national lockdown to mitigate the COVID-19 pandemic triggered a flurry of humorous exchanges among Zimbabweans on Twitter and culminated in a story published in one of the leading Zimbabwean weeklies, *The Standard*, as shown in Figure 3.8.

Beyond affirming the journalistic significance of peripheral communicative practices (albeit sometimes veiled in humour and banter that leads to 'human interest' stories in the mainstream press), the practices further give credence to Wall's view that *participatory journalism* is most successful when participation involves some 'reciprocity or forms of relational exchange between professional journalists and audiences/ amateur news participants' (Wall 2017, 135). In this new 'participatory culture' (Jenkins 2006), as seen in the example in Figure 3.8, audiences have become closely involved in the 'journalistic production cycle, and journalists find themselves in changing collaboration networks, and in roles of being a curator, interpreter, sense-maker [...] or transmedia storyteller' (Postema & Deuze 2020, 1309). The popular communicative forms complement and expand on 'issues and even more effectively express what journalists fail to communicate' (Mano 2007, 62) by drawing on local everyday 'language', which is accessible among the literate and semi-literate.

Figure 3.8 The convergence of peripheral communicative practices on social media with the mainstream press

In countries such as Zimbabwe where spaces of news engagement and information flows are restrictive or largely 'captured' by political and economic forces (Postema & Deuze 2020), ordinary citizens often engage with mainstream news and information through memes, jokes, gossip, rumours, cartoons, photoshopped images and satire circulated via SMS or platforms such WhatsApp Messenger. In some cases, these peripheral communicative forms have been used to break news or leak information deemed to be in the public interest. Thus, in contexts where invited spaces of news engagement are constrained, digitised forms of popular communication can serve as the 'voice of the voiceless by offering subtle avenues of expression' (Mano 2007, 61). Because of their 'open-ended' nature – anonymity and editable formats – jokes, memes, subvertisements and cartoons can also serve the 'journalistic' function of 'communicating daily issues in ways that challenge the powerful and give a voice to the disadvantaged' (Mano 2007, 61). The popular communicative forms have significantly lowered barriers for African publics to participate and engage directly with current affairs and mainstream news, including challenging dominant media narratives. Although the participation gap remains deep-seated between the 'haves' and the 'have nots', localised and context-specific forms of 'participatory journalism' provide an avenue through which literate, semi-literate and, in most cases, rural-based sections of society can deconstruct (and reconstruct) the elite-centric nature of the mainstream news agenda (Mare 2020). Below we give an overview of a few more examples of peripheral communicative practices that feed into our notion of *context-specific participatory practices and cultures* in Africa.

Jokes and humour

In several sub-Saharan African countries jokes and humour have emerged as popular 'interventions that [constitute] alternative media in their own right' (Willems 2011, 412). They are widely known as a response to the pervasive nature of 'public talk and oral culture' in the region but more importantly as reactions to 'attempts to crush dissent' (p. 412). Although jokes often thrive in both democratic and non-democratic contexts, it is mostly in authoritarian regimes where they are more pervasive largely due to restrictions imposed on public speech and the curtailment of freedom of expression. Given the restrictive nature of most political systems in Africa, ordinary people often use these 'digital hidden transcripts' (Mare 2020) as invented spaces of news engagement. Partly due to their anonymous origins, these localised forms of *journalism* (Mano 2007) enable people to vent, mock, and even say things that they would otherwise not say or do openly for fear of political victimisation. They also constitute communicative practices through which ordinary citizens disseminate information, engage with everyday mainstream news by poking fun at those in position of political and economic power. In the context of hyper-digitisation, jokes are increasingly interactive, elastic and viral thereby 'reverberating in countless retellings on the street and in homes' (Mano 2007, 61). Thus, the technology-mediated social practice of joking acts as a bottom-up news engagement initiative that allows people to process hard and soft news which is predominantly transmitted in a top-down fashion.

Jokes often surface on social media platforms as a reaction to mainstream news, which highlights the novel ways in which African citizens make sense of public interest information. In one typical example, in the context of biting economic challenges and persistent cash shortages in Zimbabwe, the country's education minister was quoted in the pro-government *Sunday Mail* newspaper as saying schools will have to show flexibility when it comes to demanding tuition fees from parents by accepting 'livestock [goats] as a form of payment'. In response to the statement, citizens quickly took to social media in ironic humour offering their interpretations of the minister's suggestions (see Figure 3.9). In particular, they humorously demonstrated the minister's lack of knowledge of the material welfare of Zimbabweans, especially that not everyone in Zimbabwe owns a goat, and if those with goats used them to pay school fees for one child, their stock of goats would not cover a year's school fees for one child.

Subvertisements

Like jokes, subvertisements are another form of alternative popular avenue for news engagement in Africa. It refers to 'a popular online strategy, in the form of language, picture, and animation, which comically subverts and deconstructs corporate and political advertisements' (Nomai 2008, 26). Because of the polysemic character and editable formats of news texts, pictures, videos and audios, ordinary people are deliberately turning political and corporate identities on their heads. This encompasses the digital manipulation of the popular imagery associated with a brand, slogan, or an artwork to force the reader to

Young boy playing with his school fees in Zimbabwe

When the goats heard they will be used to pay school fees.

Figure 3.9 Jokes circulated on social media after Zimbabwe's primary and secondary education minister suggested that goats could be used to pay school fees

[re]consider broader social and political issues in line with political dynamics of the day (Cammaerts 2008). Armed with digital media technologies, ordinary citizens playfully subvert a range of party slogans, political party names, manifestos, policies, programmes, draconian legislation, as well as vision and mission statements of political and corporate organisations. Viral jokes often travel from one platform to another. The unending mutation of jokes, photoshopped images and memes foregrounds the ideas that digital artefacts are often 'a perpetual accretion of little details [...] probably having neither beginning, completion nor definable limits' (Gilfillan 1935, 5).

Lower barriers of artistic expression associated with the 'social media turn' have allowed citizens to subvert official party names into obscene word play designed to demystify and ridicule governments (Mano 2007). An example of this in the South African context is when anonymous citizens subvertised the acronym for the African National Congress (ANC) to stand for 'African National Corruption', following revelations about corruption charges against top officials from the party. Similarly, the acronym of the state broadcaster in Zimbabwe, the Zimbabwe Broadcasting Corporation (ZBC) has over the years been subverted to the ZANU Broadcasting Corporation (ZBC). This is partly because the broadcaster generally covers all the activities of the ruling party, Zimbabwe African National Union Patriotic Front (ZANU-PF) in a positive light. The naming and re-naming of official acronyms and party slogans in the digital era is part of a long tradition of news engagement used by African citizens to comment on socio-economic and political affairs (Willems 2011).

Cartoons and photoshopped images

Cartoons and photoshopped images also constitute important outlets for unsolicited news engagement in Africa (Mare 2016; Hammett 2010), as genres of comic art, digital cartoons and photoshopped images ride on 'distortions and exaggerations that characteristically puncture pretension or single out vulnerable features in a target' (Farwell 1989, 9). These forms of popular communication, as Fairrington argues, 'make social and political commentary that simplifies the subtle and often complex underlying issues' (2009, 205). In Africa, the production and viral circulation of photoshopped images and cartoons has been influenced by the desire to voice unpopular socio-political opinion in the face of government crackdown on dissent (Nyamnjoh 2005; Mano 2007). Such images not only provide alternative perspectives to topical issues but also provide grounds for vigorous political and social debates on newsworthy information within the digital public sphere.

Although not everyone has the artistic skills to participate as a 'produser' (Bruns 2008), the above participatory practices and cultures also take the form of being viral distributors of content on social media. The practices tap into the viral reach and affective evaluation dimensions of social media (Alhabash & McAlister 2015; Denisova 2020). Unlike in the analogue era, these popular 'forms of journalism' have become the 'electronic word-of-mouth'(Alhabash & McAlister 2015, 1318), transmitting content in an exponentially growing way, often through the use of social media platforms which allow users to take part in distribution processes by tying content to social relations. Besides enabling people to participate in the journalistic arena through creating, modifying, repurposing and remixing mainstream news context as we have seen above, these platforms are also instrumental for breaking news and reconstituting the public fora for news engagement.

Conclusion

In this chapter, we have discussed the changing texture of participatory journalism and news engagement in the broader context of what we call the 'social media turn' in Africa. We have observed that media organisations in Africa, like their counterparts in the Global North, have embraced the affordances of social media for 'crowdsourcing journalism', interactive news engagement and viral distribution of news content across interlinked and hybrid media spaces. Most print and broadcast media organisations are encouraging their audience to engage and participate in news production through 'invited spaces of participation' (Cornwall 2002). Audiences are often *invited* to these interactive spaces of participation to share their views and engage with news content, but newsrooms are under no obligation to respond to questions and feedback. The chapter also highlights that 'unsolicited forms of participation' (Willems 2013) are dominating social media-enabled news engagement in the absence of formal invitations by media organisations and journalists. Our findings point to the normalisation of 'institutionalised interactive spaces' where audiences deliberate over news content without any input from page or account administrators. This revelation chimes with Deuze's (2003) observation that without sufficient resources or an engaged management, user-generated content initiatives are liable to wither on the vine, becoming nothing more than a fig leaf to cover the traditional 'we write, you read' dogma of modern journalism.

The chapter also demonstrates that while generic technological affordances have broadened institutionalised and uninstitutionalised forums of news engagement, there is a need to acknowledge the role of *context-specific participatory practices and cultures* through channels like pavement radio, jokes and cartoons, which point to the 'social shaping' nature of the contexts in which the technology is adopted and deployed (Bijker 1995). Thus, localised and context-specific variants of participatory journalism have been digitised enabling offline and online engagements with mainstream news content. However, despite the broadening of platforms of news engagement via the use of social media, there are still several structural impediments, which militate against the realisation of democratic and affordable participatory journalism in Africa. Some of the structural factors include the problem of the digital divide, limited digital competencies, high prices of data and unreliable electricity supply (we discuss some of these challenges in Chapter 5).

Note

1 The term *social networks* is used here in the traditional sociological sense of social interactions or relations between individuals and social groups. In contemporary times this conception is drowned out by its use in reference to social media.

4 Participatory journalism in the age of artificial intelligence, chatbots, algorithms and editorial analytics

This chapter shifts attention to audience participatory practices and automated forms of engagement associated with what we have broadly termed 'automated participatory journalism'. Although heavily skewed towards news organisations in countries whose economies are relatively stronger, such as South Africa and Namibia, and fairly patchy in other countries, these practices manifest through the strategic deployment of AI, chatbots (automated robots), algorithms and audience analytics systems in newsrooms. Recent developments suggest that human and non-human actors are increasingly implicated in online news participatory practices, especially on social media platforms.

In this chapter, we examine the extent to which developments in AI, chatbots, algorithms and analytics systems are an issue in African newsrooms. We also critically assess the implications of these tools for emerging participatory journalism cultures and practices. By investigating the role of technological *actants* (structures and actors that modify other actors through a series of actions) in user participation practices, the chapter argues that the intersection between human and non-human actors is slowly but surely reconfiguring participatory journalism in Africa. Expressed figuratively, these actants are also playing an instrumental role *in the closing of gates, guarding the gates and patrolling behind the gates.*

Automation has not only become a buzzword in the Global North, it has also become one of the key drivers of newsroom reorganisation and decentring in some African newsrooms. The concept of automation, which is at the core of the so-called Fourth Industrial Revolution[1] (4IR) refers to the technique, method, or system of operating or controlling a process by highly automatic means thereby reducing human intervention to a bare minimum. It entails the use of digital media technologies to automate newsmaking processes so that they can sequentially transition from one task to the next with minimal human intervention. It is noteworthy that the automation of news production and audience engagement in Africa and other parts of the world cannot be understood 'outside of the larger context of the digitisation of media and public life – a transition to apps, algorithms, social media and the like in ways that have transformed journalism as an institution [...]' (Broussard et al. 2019, 673).

This growing trend in the automation of newsroom tasks, workflows and processes in Africa and elsewhere is part and parcel of 'the algorithmic turn' in journalism. The shift relates to the central and strategic role of data processing and automated technologies in news production and decision making. A number of catchphrases have been coined in an effort to describe these *technology-driven* changes in journalism. These include 'automated journalism' (Carlson 2018); 'algorithmic journalism' (Dörr 2016); 'robot journalism' (Clerwall 2014); and 'computational journalism' (Young & Hermida 2014). At a general level, the monikers refer to various 'forms of algorithmic, social scientific and mathematical processes and systems for the production of news' (Young & Hermida 2014, 381). It also signifies a structural shift in the way 'stories are discovered, presented, aggregated, monetized and archived' (Cohen et al. 2011, 66). As this chapter will show, these structural changes have begun to affect news engagement cultures and practices in Africa.

For the purposes of this book, we use the term 'automated participatory practices' to refer to the processes of deploying AI-driven technologies like chatbots, algorithms, AI and analytics systems[2] to post, measure, moderate, fact-check, reply and comment on news stories with limited human effort beyond the initial programming of the software (see Chapter 1). It also encapsulates a situation where news producers are increasingly dependent on technological actants which are increasingly being designed with technical and social affordances that, among other things, facilitate automated responses on comment sections and social media platforms (Lewis 2015).

In the context of participatory journalism in Africa, the use of automated technologies is helping newsrooms to outsource their posting, moderation and fact checking of news stories sourced from social media and the Internet more broadly. These artificial 'virtual' agents are being deployed to respond to frequently asked questions (FAQs), chatting with audiences, post news stories online and fact checking hate speech. Because of the challenges associated with harmful and misleading content, newsrooms are also increasingly relying on AI-enabled content moderation systems. These systems are used to identify harmful and misleading content by following rules and interpreting many different examples of content, which is and is not harmful (Cambridge Consultants 2019).

Automated participatory journalism in the newsroom

Although most literature on 'automated journalism' has emanated from the Global North, as discussed in Chapter 1, the headwinds of automated journalistic cultures have not spared African newsrooms. In developed countries, newsrooms such as the *Washington Post, Wall Street Journal, New York Times, Bloomberg, Reuters, BBC, Huffington Post* and the *Guardian* have embraced the use of automated technologies in order to improve efficiency and effectiveness in their news production and audience engagement practices. Generally, these *'pioneers'* in automated journalism are well-funded and have invested deeply in the use of automated technologies (WAN-IFRA report 2019). On the African scene, media organisations in South Africa, Zimbabwe, Kenya and Nigeria have begun to automate their newsmaking systems as well as engagement with their audiences. These media organisations fall within what the WAN-IFRA report (2019) calls the *'experimenters'* category made up of newsrooms, which have found value in using digital technologies to automate processes and decision-making previously undertaken by humans.

Unlike traditional news engagement practices, automated systems are viewed as delivering personalised, customised and real-time news engagement experiences when compared to human moderators (Clerwall 2014). Hence, instead of relying entirely on humans to 'staff the gates' on comment sections, discussion forums on websites and social media platforms, some African media organisations are embracing automated options like analytics systems, filters, virtual assistants, algorithms and chatbots. This is in response to the shift from a one-to-many communication system to a many-to-many conversational system (Carlson 2018).

One of the most popular forms of automated algorithmic technologies in African newsrooms are chatbots (a subset of bots). Powered by algorithms, machine learning (ML)[3] and artificial intelligence, chatbots 'are software programmes designed to converse' and interact with humans via 'text-based, messenger-type interfaces' or even spoken words (Jones & Jones 2019, 1032–1033). They also provide conversational output in response, and if commanded, can sometimes also execute routine tasks like responding to questions, moderation and posting content on social media platforms. These technologies are assisting news organisations attract new audiences using conversational forms of journalism which aim to engage people 'through the leveraging of new technologies to create formats that are informal, interactive and novel' and less formal in style (Jones & Jones 2019, 1036).

Not only are African media organisations automating responses to straightforward questions when engaging with their loyal audiences, but some are even offering them suggestions based on previous behaviours and answers (Jones & Jones 2019).

Most media organisations in Africa are dependent on social media algorithms in their online news distribution and engagement processes. In the context of online distribution of news, algorithms such as Facebook's EdgeRank and Google+'s PageRank are playing an instrumental role. These technologies have proved handy in filtering, prioritising, recommending, ranking and selecting news and comments from the audiences. The reason for this is that algorithms can be manipulated to an extent that is not possible with human beings.

AI as a branch of computer science concerned with the simulation of human intelligence has also permeated some African newsrooms thereby reconfiguring the production and distribution of news content. In the Global North, AI is being used as a solution to help personal content discovery across broadcast and linear channels, catch-up services and content from TV apps like *Netflix* and *Videoland* and short-form content from YouTube (Broussard et al. 2019). Machine learning (ML) and deep learning[4] (DL), which are subsets of AI have led to 'the training of machines to learn from data, recognise patterns and make subsequent judgments, with little to no human intervention' (Broussard et al. 2019, 673). *The Washington Post* deploys ModBot, a software application that utilises AI to moderate comments. This technology uses ML to automatically filter comments that require human moderation, flag stories that require real-time monitoring, and approve or delete comments based on the newspaper's discussion policy (Broussard et al. 2019).

In the developed economies, these technologies have assisted newsrooms to semi-automate or even fully automate some of their day-to-day tasks like finding stories, doing photography, videography work, moderating online comments, editing and publishing their work on social media platforms. Compared to manual moderation by human beings, AI can be used to improve the pre-moderation stage and flag content for review by humans thereby increasing moderation accuracy (Cambridge Consultants 2019). It can also be implemented to synthesise training data to improve the effectiveness of human moderators by prioritising content to be reviewed by them based on its potential level of harmfulness or the level of uncertainty from an automated moderation stage (Cambridge Consultants 2019).

Automated participatory journalism in Africa has also been significantly influenced by the use of analytics systems. Analytics systems such as Disqus, Chartbeat, Facebook Insights and Google

Analytics are supporting African newsrooms in packaging and distributing online news content. The tools are particularly used to measure audience engagement and make decisions on whether to produce certain content, where to position articles on the website or social media and when to publish it online (Moyo, D. et al. 2019). Using metrics, which refers to units of measurement that reflect a specific element of audience behaviour (e.g. page views, click rates, browse through rates, likes, comments and so forth), media organisations in Africa can undertake granular news performance appraisals (Blanchett Neheli 2018). Editors and journalists are increasingly monitoring metrics to determine how much traffic the chatbot directs back to the website, which can then be used to inform further work on the platform. These analytics systems have enabled media organisations to package news content, which are likely to promote solicited and unsolicited news engagements.

The rest of the chapter critically examines the implications of deploying technological actants like analytics systems, AI, chatbots and algorithms in a bid to enrich participatory journalistic practices. We demonstrate that automated participatory journalism has opened up more opportunities for human and non-human actors to collaborate and complement each other. We argue that although technological actants act like self-contained processes or 'black boxes', they are in fact socially constructed (Bijker 1995) and thus open to negotiation.

On the flip side, we demonstrate how the adoption of automated systems in participatory journalism has also partly contributed to the proliferation and amplification of fake news, misinformation, disinformation, trolling and rumour mongering in Africa (see Chapter 5). As a result, there have been loud calls in scholarly and policy circles for the auditing of algorithms, the designing of ethical newsbots and the deployment of effective rights-based moderation practices. Our overarching argument is that online participatory cultures powered by 'conversational agents' also present systemic challenges in terms of realising authentic or 'organic' news engagement, fostering civil discourse and promoting the ideal of the public interest, especially in the light of extant questions on digital literacy and the general impact of the digital divide on the African continent.

How technological 'actants' are shaping and influencing practices in newsrooms

AI and audience participation

Although the appropriation of AI in journalism has gained more traction in Europe and North America (Broussard et al. 2019), some media houses in South Africa have started to deploy these tools in reporting, content creation, distribution and audience interaction. In the context of audience participation, AI is considered effective in helping moderators to filter UGC on comments spaces at a faster rate. It is used in efforts to identify toxic comments that can undermine a civil exchange of ideas (we discuss AI-driven content moderation later). Interviews with online editors in South Africa highlighted some of these developments, particularly how newsrooms are experimenting with AI software to enrich their audience participation cultures and practices, as the Online Media Editor of *Times Media Group* explained: 'We are [...] now employing AI software that analyzes our website and social media platform analytics, then automates our social media posts and publication schedule to optimise it for maximum engagement and traffic referral'.

Some editors saw AI as helping to 'decongest and free time' for their production teams to concentrate more on the quality of their product, as the Digital Media Editor at *Tiso Blackstar* (now *Arena Media Group*) put it: 'Because of the new software we have acquired our web production teams have more time to focus on the professional presentation of our digital content instead of spending hours creating, scheduling and responding to social media posts manually'. A Digital Editor at the *Independent Newspapers* similarly highlighted that AI is helping reporters to tailor and 'personalise content based on where audiences live and other demographics, such as age, gender and so on' than would otherwise be possible in the intense deadline-driven daily routines. In other words, AI is making up for the limitations of humans, including 'human error', as explained by the Digital Media Editor at *Media24*: 'We're using AI to study the behavioral patterns of our audience, to [...] schedule social media content and articles to reduce the workload and time journalists and content producers spend doing these tasks manually'.

From the above, it is evident that leading media houses in South Africa are adopting AI-driven technologies as a potential way to lessen the burden of managing their audience engagement platforms, particularly social media and comment sections. It is important, however, to highlight that because of lack of capacity in the development of applications, newsrooms in South Africa are relying on proprietary third-party AI software from the Global North. With the exception of *Media24*, which has a fully assembled team of engineers responsible for developing customised and personalised apps, our study revealed that some newsrooms lacked in-house capacity, hence the overreliance on local and international vendors. Several digital media editors confirmed this trend where

South African media organisations work with international vendors, especially from Russia, Ukraine and the United States of America to buy state of the art AI software for their newsrooms.

Unlike their neighbours in South Africa, respondents from Zimbabwe's Alpha Media Holdings (AMH) and Zimpapers respectively highlighted that they have not yet fully embraced AI software for online participatory practices. For instance, AMH's Online Editor had this to say:

> Instead of using an AI related software, we used the automated responses option on our Facebook page. It has a programmed message, which says 'we will get back to you soon'. We also used a word filtering system that allowed us to flag politically incorrect words.

A senior journalist at Zimpapers pointed to an even less sophisticated scenario:

> [...] at the moment we don't use any AI software for our audience participation. Like other media houses we rely on Disqus, which is a content management system. It allows us to create, edit, organise and publish our content online [...].

From this, it is evident that while AI is redefining audience participation dynamics in Western newsrooms, there is still a long way to go until there is a widespread adoption in Africa. While South African newsrooms are leading in experimenting with the use of AI to engage with their audiences, it remains to be seen how other resource-constrained newsrooms in Africa are adapting to the opportunities afforded by AI.

Social media algorithms and news engagement

As discussed in Chapter 3, the use of social media platforms as outlets for online news engagement has become more popular than comment sections on news websites across the globe. The coming in of interactive social media platforms has made it easier for news organisations to outsource commenting, sharing and recommending to third party platforms. In keeping with their counterparts in Europe (Jones & Jones 2019), some news organisations in Africa are using social media to drive website traffic through referrals and pushing offsite traffic through native formats and distributed content. Because of these reconfigurations in the venues of audience participation, it is not far-fetched to surmise that social media engagement has not escaped the unpredictable influences of algorithms, especially in terms of sharing, recommending and commenting on news content. It is in the interest of social media companies and news outlets to steer their users towards 'trending stories' that promote high levels of news engagement.

Facebook and Twitter algorithms play a critical role in filtering, ranking, sorting, searching, prioritising, selecting and recommending news content to audiences. The opposite is equally true – algorithms also marginalise news content as well as render certain kinds of news engagement invisible. As Ndlela (2020) observes, despite the powerful role that social media algorithms play in shaping and defining digital media ecologies, their quasi-autonomous logic and practice remains largely opaque. Thus, opening up the 'black box' of algorithms has proved to be a tall order for editors and journalists in Africa.

Interviews with some of the journalists working at the coalface of digital newsroom operations in South Africa, Namibia and Zimbabwe indicated that newsrooms invest time and resources in trying to understand the logic of algorithms and their implications for audience participation. Journalists highlighted that they follow updates on changes effected to algorithms by social media companies in order to leverage them for their own news distribution and engagement purposes. Some of the journalists we interviewed explained this as follows:

> For the past three years we have focused on the analysis that centred on what metrics on SimilarWeb and Google analytics were telling us. I would say our knowledge of how social media algorithms work is rather limited. However, we paid a lot of attention to data emerging from tech sites writing about algorithms.
>
> (Online Editor, AMH, Zimbabwe)

> Our team of experts are always on top of their game researching on these things. They advise editors and journalists on how to take advantage of the workings of certain algorithms. We know for a fact that images, GIFs and short videos attract a lot of traffic and engagements on our platforms. So we try to build our online content around this kind of business intelligence.
>
> (Digital Media Editor, *Media24*, South Africa)

From the interview extracts above, it seems clear that social media algorithms are seriously implicated in journalistic decision making. Like human editors, algorithms decide what information should be made visible to the audience and what information should not (Mare

2016; Ndlela 2020). For example, Facebook's EdgeRank uses an automated and predetermined selection mechanism to establish relevancy (most interesting) on its News Feed (Bucher 2017). It has since updated its algorithms to prioritise posts that spark conversations and meaningful interactions between people. Similarly, Online Editors across newsrooms note that Twitter algorithms emphasise *recency* (how recently a tweet was published); the *type of media* a user includes in the Tweet, such as images, videos and GIFs; how active a user is; and *engagement* (how many retweets, clicks, favourites and impressions a tweet receives). In general, there is acknowledgement of the fact that social media algorithms affect the visibility or invisibility of news and information. They equally contribute to the viral distribution of news content 'far beyond algorithm-based platforms to non-algorithm-based applications like WhatsApp' (Ndlela 2020, 21). As discussed in Chapter 3, viral information often finds itself dominating 'pavement radio' discussions in Africa.

Chatbots and participatory journalism

Over the years, chatbots have evolved from simply being able to 'automate headline delivery to the delivery of news according to a conversational format within the context of private messaging services' (Ford & Hutchinson 2019, 1013). With advances in artificial intelligence, chatbots have become smarter and relatively cheap to build and implement. Advanced newsbots are capable of responding to 'user input by simulating how a human would behave as a partner in a conversation' (Ford & Hutchinson 2019, 1013). As Keller and Klinger (2019) observe, bots can automatically produce messages, post in online forums, and interact with social media users through likes and comments, advocate ideas, act as followers (fake accounts) and even share social media contributions. Research has also shown that when used correctly chatbots can reach new audiences by building a more informal, intimate relationship with users (Lokot & Diakopoulos 2016).

Because of their conversational capabilities, well-resourced African media organisations are embracing proprietary and non-proprietary chatbots into their audience participation toolkits. Online editors of media houses in South Africa, Namibia and Zimbabwe revealed that rather than simply relying on content management systems (CMS) and filter search interfaces, they are increasingly using third party chatbots to interact with their audiences on public and private social media platforms. Third party platforms such as Chartfuel, Botpress, Ras Webchat, Bot Content and Fb Botmill make it possible even for resource-constrained newsrooms to launch bots without writing code, a limited technical skill in most African newsrooms. A webmaster at the *Windhoek Observer* in Namibia noted that some media houses in the country 'are using third party platforms to automate their commenting and posting of online content' although the general trend leans more on manual 'posting and interactions with loyal readers'.

Unlike in the Global North, where media organisations are generally financially endowed and more technically adept, which allows them to build their own news bots from scratch, in Africa, as our study shows, limited technical and financial resources are impeding the development and launch of locally designed chatbots. For instance, in America and Europe, *Quartz* has rolled out a chatbot that enables users to text questions about news events, people, or places, and the app replies with content it believes is relevant to them. Thus, rather than relying entirely on human to human interactions (H-to-H), newsrooms in the Global North are replacing that equation with human and non-human (H-to-nH) engagements. As seen earlier, bots are able to generate messages, post in online forums, as well as interact with social media users through automated responses (Keller & Klinger 2019). However, most news organisations in the Global South are still relying on manual responses largely reflecting lack of AI and digital competencies as well as limited financial resources.

Editorial analytics and news engagement

In the context of 'creative and quantified audiences' (Carlson 2018), editors and journalists in Africa are no longer relying on the old mass media conception of audiences. The adoption of proprietary analytics systems such as Disqus, Chartbeat, Facebook Insights and Google Analytics has enabled media organisations in Africa to interact with 'visible' audiences both in terms of aggregated (monitoring and audience measurement) and singular feedback (contributions of individual users). As Zamith (2018, 418) observes, 'audiences and quantification are playing far more prominent roles in news production than in the past'. Gone are the days of the 'invisible audiences', whereby African media organisations used to make decisions on news production, distribution and consumption based on pure gut feeling. Thus, the interactions between journalists and audiences have shifted from a previously detached transactional relationship to an interactional exchange.

Technological actants like analytics systems have allowed media organisations to accurately measure the performance of their online news stories as well as assess the feedback from their audiences in real time (Zamith 2018). Thus, participatory journalism at the level of editorial metrics (e.g. social media comments, likes, retweets, shares, recommendations, followership and fandom) has become a 'measurable' phenomenon 'capable of providing real-time, individualisable, quantitative data about audience consumption practices' (Carlson 2018, 406). Interviews with editors in Zimbabwe, South Africa and Kenya revealed that audience analytics are being used to monitor, track and interact with their audiences.

Because of the proliferation of audience analytics, news organisations in Africa have access to a wide range of big and thick data about their loyal audiences. Most news organisations are now able to use this data to inform their day-to-day newsmaking decisions as well as engage in what Blanchett Neheli (2018) refers to as 'promotional gatekeeping' and 'deselection' of poorly performing news content. In other words, technological actants are providing real-time quantitative data about audiences while permitting new modes of engagement and accountability (Moyo, D. et al. 2019). Analytics tools have made it cheaper and easier for media organisations in Africa to automatically quantify editorial metrics such as likes, views, shares, clicks, comments and retweets.

The deployment of analytics systems in Kenya, Zimbabwe and South Africa suggests significant alteration in the ways in which newsrooms measure the dynamics of news engagement on their websites and social media platforms. While readers' comments on websites and social media platforms have traditionally provided journalists with story ideas, as seen in Chapters 2 and 3, the overreliance on audience analytics has been accompanied by clickbait headlines, strategic manipulation of social media algorithms, distribution of news that interests the public rather than what is in the public interest and constant reworking of online news introductions. This fascination with measurable aspects of news has spawned the emergence of what Moyo, D. et al. (2019) describe as 'analytics-driven journalism' in Africa.

Interviews with journalists and editors revealed that the major benefits of using analytics systems such as Facebook Insights, Twitter Analytics and YouTube Analytics include enhanced understanding of their audiences and how they interact with their content. They spoke about the numbers of 'eyeballs' attracted to each story, how long they stay on each story, and how far they scroll down a story. Real-time data culled from social media platforms also helped newsrooms to understand the nature of devices their audiences use (i.e. mobile phones, tablets or desktops), and their geographical location. Respondents across a number of African countries highlighted that audience metric data enabled their newsroom to identify stories that are trendy and sought after and those that are not performing well in real time so that they can make necessary adjustments. As one Digital Media Editor at the Nation Media Group in Kenya explained:

> Analytics systems have broadened my sense of audience research. Because of the many data points involved, it is easy, for instance, to know what men of a particular age, residing in a particular area, are interested in. By mapping such audiences, I am able to keep tabs on their reading trends and appeals, and hence broaden my coverage to include them and the many others occupying different zones in the digital sphere.

Journalists highlighted the collective strengths of the analytics tools noted above in providing key insights into audience behaviour online, including the type of news they follow and the amount of time they spend per story. Analytics systems were described as enabling editors to measure the performance of each story in real time, and where necessary to make adjustments. Our data further revealed that it has also become common practice for headlines and introductions to be tweaked to generate more traffic to specific stories, based on performance data drawn from analytics systems. One journalist at *CNBC Africa* explained this practice as follows:

> These tools have helped us understand the kind of audiences we have. As a business channel, through analytics, we have realised our followers also like political stories and that is influencing our content strategy. Some political stories generate more clicks compared to business stories. In Southern Africa, Zimbabwe and Zambia are leading on political clicks.

Another respondent from the *Nation Media Group* observed:

> Stories that perform well online are sometimes a pointer to a reporting gap, or a specific interest that could be seasonal or evergreen. We use data from such stories to discuss story angles and day-two approaches for the paper the following day. The data is also crucial in determining which stories need a rethink, which ones need better presentation next time (a video or extra photo, perhaps?), or which ones we should never have touched in the first place.

Instead of simply promoting engaged participatory journalism in Africa, it is arguable that editorial metrics data have become the key to unlocking the advertising dollar online, apart from aiding editorial decision-making. This chimes with Willems' (2013) argument that the adoption of audience participation is closely linked to the commercial imperatives of media organisations.

Thus, participatory journalism in the African context has been significantly transformed by the use of analytics systems. However, relying on audience metrics to make sense of online audiences is not without negative implications. These include the push by some media organisations towards churning out clickbait headlines and introductions, the proliferation of sensationalised content and even fake news in order to attract more clicks, views and shares. In several interviews, the idea of journalists being directly involved in the 'marketing' of their own stories and interacting directly with their audiences was recurrent, thus illustrating a shift in journalistic roles and responsibilities in the newsrooms. Most journalists in South Africa and Kenya, for instance, indicated that they are expected to have professional social media accounts and emails for promoting their stories and engaging directly with the audiences although, as we observe in Chapter 5, this presents its own normative challenges in terms of diminishing personal boundaries and privacy.

The emerging fascination with metrics has also led to a growing tendency to focus on stories that elicit high levels of engagement through 'clicks', 'likes', and 'shares' in most African newsrooms. This, however, means that stories that matter in terms of building an engaged citizenship but whose metric value is low tend to get marginalised. The downside to this, predictably, is that media organisations in Africa could easily fall into the trap of using headlines for clickbait in a bid to capture the elusive digital advertising dollar. In order to foster a culture of 'participative gatekeeping', Blanchett Neheli (2018) advocates for the institutionalisation of transparent feedback mechanisms, whether through social or in-person interactions.

Automated UGC moderation

Because of the large amounts of comments that newsrooms in Africa have to deal with on their websites and social media platforms, as discussed in Chapters 2 and 3, they are beginning to appropriate technological actants as moderators. In general, there are two AI-driven moderation strategies adopted by news media organisations. These are pre- and post-moderation strategies. Pre-moderation refers to a practice where uploaded content is moderated prior to publication, typically using automated systems (Cambridge Consultants 2019). Post- or reactive-moderation is when content is moderated after it has been published and flagged by other users or automated processes as potentially harmful (Cambridge Consultants 2019). Thus, while editors have broadly preferred a non-moderation approach combined with loose forms of content restriction or filtering as discussed in Chapter 2, AI's ability to filter a lot of data on comments sections has seen newsrooms increasingly deploying AI-driven machines as *patrollers of gates, gate enforcers* and *gate guards* (Thurman et al. 2016) on social media platforms and websites. This is generally in line with the 'automation turn' in the newsroom as discussed earlier. The pervasive nature of 'invited spaces of participation' (Cornwall 2002) has pushed media organisations in Africa to come up with a number of moderation strategies in order to secure their *virtual gates* on social media platforms and website comment sections.

In some extreme cases, moderation strategies have taken the form of *total closure of the gates* although in most cases, as we note above, this has simply entailed *guarding the gates* or *patrolling behind the gates* (Hermida & Thurman 2008; Thurman et al. 2016). The first strategy entails shutting down the comment sections or disabling interactive features that allow users to comment on news websites of social media platforms. In Zimbabwe and Kenya, Online Editors pointed out that they have resorted to occasionally deleting and moving to the spam section harmful, hurtful and misleading content using Disqus as a way of curbing the spreading of uncivil discourse and hate speech. In the broader scheme of things, this highlights that news media professionals in Africa, as elsewhere, have been rather restrictive and are hesitant to allow users to participate. For instance, the Online Editor at AMH in Zimbabwe stated:

> We depend on filters and WordPress basically. Although I feel it is not effective. At some point we tried Disqus but it was cumbersome for our [readers] to comment. We realised that the comments section brought in a lot of traffic. We then decided to filter words that we felt were politically incorrect over time. We employed an intern who would follow up on all comments that would have been filtered into the spam section. At times genuine comments without any hurtful speech are flagged as bad comments and are categorised as spam.

Zimpapers' Online Editor pointed to an even less sophisticated scenario:

> [...] we use Disqus for comments moderation, but we make manual interventions with regards to 'unfavourable' comments. With Disqus we can only blacklist foul words in English, but

native words we cannot deal with them that way. Also, people know how to navigate around such software and can always bypass by way of disguising certain words, e.g. *ass* can be written as *@$$*.

It is clear from the last quotation that users are not deterred nor are they discouraged by the barriers set by automated technology, rather they develop approaches to resist and negotiate techno-moderation systems used by media organisations. This further points to the 'social shaping' of technology use, which is rooted in individual and collective agency in navigating technological barriers. Thus, to use Berger's terms, African online audiences always *adapt* and *learn*, they possess 'internal creativity, strengths and adaptations' (2005, 1).

Furthermore, the two Zimbabwean cases above point to the disproportionate levels in the extent to which AI is being adopted and deployed to shape audience engagement and participation in Africa. It is also evident from the interview extracts that the two main news organisations in Zimbabwe are still using CMS and open source technologies like WordPress and Disqus to deal with UGC. Unlike most CMS on the market, WordPress requires nothing beyond a domain and a hosting service. Disqus has in-built automated pre-moderation controls for flagging comments based on links and user reputation. It also has self-moderation tools such as user blocking and comment flagging.

Our findings in Zimbabwe highlighted the challenges of using Western designed software in non-English speaking contexts where the general public often use indigenous languages or vernacular to engage with news online. Besides demonstrating the creativity of audiences in terms of circumventing the automated moderation systems, it foregrounds the limitations of relying on technologies from the Global North without contextual domestication and localisation. Additionally, unfavourable comments are not only about hurtful, harmful and misleading content but also about content that goes against the ideologies of the political and economic elites and thus requiring manual or traditional moderation. As one senior journalist at Zimpapers observed:

> There are two perspectives from which we moderate the comments [...] you will notice that of late, we have kind of slid back to old ways of dealing with comments which are ideologically against the grain. Those would require manual intervention, whilst from a technical perspective, you can deal with both types of comments by way of blacklisting offensive words regardless of who they are targeting. *But you may also want to learn that the current editor is so much against any kind of disapproval of the status quo [...] and*

> *my fear is this is going to undo all the progress we had made towards exploitation of user generated content and reader feedback.*
>
> (emphasis added)

It can thus be deduced that whilst technological systems are important for efficient and timely moderation of content, there are also political and ideological considerations, which are used to decide on permissible and impermissible forms of speech online. In order for automated moderation systems to work effectively, there is need for 'dark' content to be properly defined. Thus, technological actants alone are not enough in terms of ensuring politically correct moderation practices and cultures are adhered to.

Interviews with Online Editors in Namibia also highlighted the shift towards the embracing of AI-driven technological actants like filters and a range of CMS. Instead of employing full-time page administrators responsible for curating, moderating and responding to audience feedback, one respondent highlighted the following:

> There is a marked change in the last couple of years. Since we don't have full-time staff to look through our comment sections and social media sites, we have resorted to using filters or content management systems such as WordPress. Sometimes we rely on our users to flag things like hate speech, foul language and defamation on our pages.
>
> (Online Editor, *Windhoek Observer*, Namibia)

This further supports the view made earlier that some media organisations in Africa are relying on filters and CMS to undertake pre-moderation of readers' comments. In view of the moderation strategies identified by Thurman et al. (2016), this relates to *guarding the gates*, at least in part.

As part of *closing the gates*, some newsrooms in South Africa, Zimbabwe and Kenya highlighted that they systematically block well-known trolls – participants who deliberately sow discord by posting inflammatory and digressive, extraneous, or off-topic messages in an online community. Similar measures were taken against 'government, military or political party teams committed to manipulating public opinion over social media' (Bradshaw & Howard 2018, 24), all commonly referred to as *cyber-troops*. Other newsrooms adopted the strategy of *patrolling behind the gates* (moderating comments after publication). This is generally evident on social media platforms like Facebook, Twitter and YouTube where user comments considered to be in bad taste are deleted, hidden or even blocked. Although the typology advanced by Thurman et al. (2016) did not explicitly address the issue of automated or AI-driven moderation practices, it can be argued that these technological actants have been implicated in the closing of gates, guarding the gates and patrolling behind the gates in the African news media landscape.

Evidently the discussion above points to a shift towards *technology-dependent moderation strategies* in some African newsrooms. While we cannot conclude that machines have taken over from human moderators, this chapter suggests that indeed repetitive and routine tasks are increasingly being outsourced to programmed filters, algorithms and CMS. The rationale for these automated moderation strategies is that most media organisations in Africa primarily offer 'below the lines' audience participation. However, because most newsrooms survive on shoestring budgets and employ temporary sit-in correspondents, there has been a realisation that offering a platform for comments is not part of their core mandate. Whereas some media organisations like *News24* in South Africa have totally closed their comment sections, others have reacted by steering their audiences towards social media platforms. As Fiegerman (2014) surmises, compared to comment sections on newspaper websites, audience participation on social media is self-policed by participants who occasionally weed out offensive contributions. The assumption here is that comments on Facebook can be read by all Facebook users and are linked to personal accounts. For Hille and Bakker (2014, 563), this loss of anonymity ensures that Facebook commenters become more hesitant about posting abusive and offensive comments.

Conclusion

This chapter has explored the implications of the appropriation of automated journalistic participatory practices in Africa. While the deployment of AI systems for audience participation is beginning to take shape in selected newsrooms, the chapter has shown that there are still several structural factors militating against the complete adoption of these actants. The limitations of AI skills and resources hinder the 'democratisation' of AI-derived benefits in most newsrooms. This has resulted in the deployment of automated applications being heavily tilted in favour of well-funded news organisation in countries like South Africa, Kenya and Namibia. News organisations in the majority of African countries are still relying on basic filters and CMS to undertake routine tasks like scheduling posts, posting and responding to audience feedback. Equally, because of limited in-house capacity, the bulk of African media organisations are depending on local and international vendors to acquire chatbots and AI technologies. Others are using open source software technologies in order to cut down on costs. This creates a lot of problems because imported technologies are programmed to deal with illegal and uncivil content based on the cultural and linguistic input of the designers rather than the intended users. As we have demonstrated in this chapter, it is important to consider the geographical variations of content and how it is bound to be interpreted. In short, content which is illegal and uncivil in one country may be legal in another (Cambridge Consultants 2019, 31). Our interviews revealed that there are no newsroom-specific community standards which allow for a consistent and proportionate enforcement of standards.

With regards to analytics systems, the chapter has demonstrated that such tools have enabled newsrooms in Africa to harvest granular data on the online behavioural patterns of their audiences. This metric data has assisted newsrooms to package content that leverages audience needs and preferences in order to achieve high levels of news engagement. We have shown that both technological actants and human actors are still playing significant roles in the context of *automated* participatory journalism in Africa. While we agree with many other scholars (Hermida & Thurman 2008; Thurman et al. 2016) that human actors continue to play a role in terms of engaging with audiences and moderating online content, we are cognisant of the fact that technological actants are complementing and in some cases even supplanting human labour. Although most of the software in operation is useful in terms of handling traditional content formats (for instance, text), there are no live content moderation tools on the market to deal with deep fakes, memes, gifs, live chats and videos (Cambridge Consultants 2019). However, automated moderation raises questions about the ability of machines to make ethical decisions on content. It also brings to the fore the issue of the kind of values that undergird algorithmic decision-making. We explore some of these questions in the next chapter, which focuses on the normative and ethical dilemmas associated with participatory journalism in Africa.

Notes

1 A catchphrase that represents a new chapter in human development, enabled by advances in technology commensurate with those of the first, second and third industrial revolutions (Schwab 2015).
2 Analytics systems are platforms specifically designed to aggregate, display and assist in the reporting of audience data (for instance, Chartbeat, Google Analytics, Omniture and so forth) (Blanchett Neheli 2018).

3 A method of data analysis that automates analytical model building. It is a branch of AI based on the idea that systems can learn from data, identify patterns and make decisions with minimal human intervention.

4 A subset of machine learning in AI that has networks capable of learning unsupervised from data that is unstructured or unlabelled.

5 Unsettling changes, normative dilemmas and ethical challenges

While participatory journalism in Africa can be seen as broadly signalling 'an expansion of journalistic capabilities' (Campbell 2004, 245) as well as highlighting the sheer endless possibilities emerging with the era of interactive digital technologies, it also ushers in new threats and entrenches 'age old' challenges and normative dilemmas to the practice of journalism (Mare et al. 2019). As Robinson aptly puts it, '[n]ew demands in long-established [journalistic] cultures inevitably create tensions' (2011, 1126) which threaten traditional normative standards and practices. In short, participatory journalism has become a 'prime site of the normative crisis' (Duff 2008) facing African journalism in the digital era as new ethical problems emerge and old ethical concerns take on new meaning (Pavlik 2000).

This chapter explores some of the unsettling ethical disruptions and challenges emerging with the normalisation of digital participatory practices in both professional and everyday life. It puts the spotlight on how these developments are contributing to a transformation of journalism and its practice at a number of levels, including the relations between journalists and sources, the structuring of everyday routines and the implications of these changes for the nature of news. The chapter follows Alistair Duff's (2008) advice that in the so-called 'information society' era, which is characterised by the rapid proliferation of new digital technologies and their impact on society, 'attention should increasingly be focused upon [the ensuing] normative dimensions', which relate to the disruption of the very nature of journalism itself and its core production practices (Fenton 2010). As Deuze puts it, we can now certainly identify the effects of interactive participatory practices on 'the profession and its culture(s)' (2003, 203).

While some of the ongoing concerns relate to the contemporary crisis facing journalism globally, especially in the Global North, where digital participatory cultures have long been seen as 'redefining and rethinking "traditional" journalism' (Deuze & Dimoudi 2002, 86), we also highlight the particularities of the lasting changes to the day-to-day newsmaking routines and practices. These contextually rooted developments point to the deeper implications of the socio-economic, political and cultural contexts in which participatory journalism emerges. On the one hand, *ethical and normative dilemmas* revolve around the proliferation of 'fake news', hate speech, the challenges of verifying and 'gatekeeping' volumes of UGC, the blurring of private and professional lives and the invasion of personal privacy for both journalists and ordinary citizens. On the other, interactive digital platforms are implicated in the *redefinition of news and the disruption of institutionalised newsroom routines* as seen through the dearth of shoe-leather reporting and the inadvertent advancement of an 'elite news culture' (Mabweazara 2011) that ignores large parts of human existence outside digital spaces thus giving new meanings to news access. These challenges and modifications to journalism have also been linked to automated participatory practices associated with AI.

Understanding how participatory journalism is transforming the practice of journalism in Africa requires a brief contextualisation of contemporary scholarship on interactive digital technologies and journalism practice on the continent.

African 'participatory journalism' research: Between proponents and apostates

Research on the impact of digital technologies on journalism in Africa to date can be loosely divided between researchers who see the technologies as a 'goldmine' that presents African journalists with new opportunities for improved practice, and those who see an uncomfortable professional transition in which new practices threaten established normative traditions of journalism (Chari 2009; Kwet 2019; Mare et al. 2019). Focusing on the distinctive technological attributes of the Internet and social media[1] on journalism practice, some enthusiasts emphasise the centrality of the interactivity of online editions of African newspapers and their social media platforms, which collectively allow users to comment, give feedback or vote on controversial issues (Paterson 2013; Suau & Pere 2014). This group of scholars contend that the interactivity of new digital technologies has enabled journalists in Africa to move closer to directly engaging with readers, thus '*reinvigorating*' journalism and 'reconnecting it with a disillusioned readership' (Mabweazara 2015a, 13, emphasis in the original). In this sense, interactive and participatory cultures are seen as 'shaking up traditional journalism and turning journalists back to the 'orthodoxy' of the profession. [Thereby] giving journalism *renewed human perspective* that has been lost over the years' (Mabweazara 2014, 76, emphasis in the original).

For some, this ability to engage with news and with other news consumers is giving readers in Africa a greater influence over the material reported in newspapers while at the same time providing journalists with an opportunity to access ideas and leads from readers (Moyo, D. 2009). The appropriation of the mobile phone, which is widely touted as transforming Africa's communication landscape, has also assumed a central position in the romanticisation of digital participatory practices on the continent. It is seen as critical in facilitating 'professional journalism and [enabling] citizens to participate in the process of reporting' (Verclas & Mechael 2008, 8) and directly engaging with news. The SMS application, in particular, was once described as 'the most potent tool' (Moyo, D. 2009, 556) because of its reliability and affordability compared to making a phone call before it was replaced by WhatsApp. Crowdsourcing and the enabling of citizens 'to submit eyewitness reports' via SMS or WhatsApp messages, especially in moments of crisis such as 'election related political violence' (Willems & Mano 2016, 6), are also noted as positive developments.

However, among the more guarded group of African digital media scholars, the foregoing celebratory views have been approached with some caution or outright scepticism (Mare, 2014). This group of scholars emphasise the challenges and threats that digital technologies pose for journalism standards and its practice. Chari (2009) for example, argues that the euphoria associated with the Internet in Africa has tended to eclipse the ethical dilemmas and challenges associated with the medium – '[j]ournalists no longer feel compelled to adhere to the ethical canons' (2009, 1) of the profession. Factual errors, fabrications and copyright infringements have become much more prevalent than before' (Chari 2009, 1). Similarly, Mudhai and Nyabuga (2001), writing just after the turn of the millennium, posit that the difficulties faced in trying to authenticate online sources raises questions of news accuracy and credibility. These views echo misgivings expressed by Kasoma in the mid-1990s in his argument that the 'the information superhighway[2] has made journalists practise their profession in a hurry as they strive to satisfy the world's craving for more and quicker news' (1996, 95), resulting in 'the humaneness of journalism' increasingly giving way to the expediencies of cut-throat financial competition.

Contemporary African digital media scholarship highlights several other 'newer' challenges and normative dilemmas that point to the increasingly sophisticated nature of digital technologies and their entanglement with socio-political dynamics and material circumstances in which they are appropriated. In discussing the contemporary problems facing journalism in sub-Saharan Africa, Mare et al. (2019, 2) observe that the digital transformation of the news media ecosystem, which has resulted in low barriers to media and artistic expression, 'provide a fertile ground for the [mass] production, [circulation] and consumption of fake news and cyber-propaganda'. Gatekeeping practices such as rigorous verification and fact-checking traditionally associated with legacy media are struggling to cope with the mass production and circulation of content (Mare et al. 2019). For some observers, this has resulted in the increasing adoption of automated technologies including AI and editorial analytics systems to try to make sense of complex information flows as well as manage the influx of fake news, hate speech and cyber propaganda. These technologies are described as 'deeply insidious' and 'substrate' – broadly invisible to everyday people (Drabinski 2018). They are seen as the substratum of 'dark forms of participation' (Quandt 2018) and with no capacity to make ethical judgements. In the same vein, some scholars highlight how automation and other interactive technologies serve to entrench inequalities of news access thus pointing to the illusion of participatory journalism as horizontal and equalising. These scholars explore what is hidden from view by AI and algorithmic manipulations by the all-powerful platform companies (Kwet 2019), consequently calling for 'a closer inspection of what values are prioritised in [...] automated decision-making systems' (Noble 2018, 1).

Some scholars confront the 'fantasy of the internet as equalizing device' (Noble 2018, 1), arguing that the production of online content and the participation of citizens on news websites is controlled by a privileged elite who are predominantly male (Brinkman et al. 2011). Social topics discussed on websites (including social media) are seen as not only concentrating on the subjects and interests of the privileged class but as products of elite contributors with unrestricted access to digital technologies. Equally, the disproportionate access to digital technologies in most African countries is perceived as not only cementing 'established relations between elite forces and newsmakers' but also restricting the 'scope of the stories covered to the interests and agenda set by those with regular access' (Mabweazara 2011, 64) and knowledge of how to effectively use the technologies. It is in this light that Brinkman et al. (2011, 248) contend that the notion that 'the Internet offers a voice to the marginalised [and] allows for democratization through popular participation' must be reconsidered. This is partly because in such a context, 'participation by the poor classes is undermined by a combined effect of weak critical (media) literacies and a poor sense of civic virtue and responsibility' (Moyo, L 2020, 283). Besides the challenges associated with the digital divide and digital literacies, researchers have also raised questions around the increasingly sophisticated surveillance cultures of social media, diminishing spatial boundaries and the invasion of privacy (Mabweazara 2013; Kwet 2019).

The differences of opinion among researchers above highlight the sophisticated nature of the so called 'digital revolution' and its impact on journalism in Africa. The rest of the chapter discusses the *ethical threats, challenges* and *normative dilemmas* emerging with the era of participatory journalism.

'Dark forms of participation' and emerging professional dilemmas

Social media, which was once reified for its assumed democratisation potential, is now being re-evaluated for its negative social impact (Curran 2016). Thus, rather than simplistically viewing social media as broadening audience participation platforms, there is talk of what Thorsten Quandt (2018) frames as '*dark forms of participation*'. This concept highlights the bleak flip side to participatory journalism, which is characterised by the circulation of harmful or hateful messages, incivility, trolling, large-scale misinformation and disinformation through comment sections and social media pages of established media organisations (Quandt 2018). These dark forms of participation also include 'destructive engagement, involuntary imposition, silencing and self-censoring, and exclusion' (Carpentier et al. 2019, 19). In the sections that follow we discuss the common forms of 'dark participation' in sub-Saharan Africa and the complexities around verifying and managing online UGC.

Disinformation and fake news

Disinformation is often used to denote the deliberate (often orchestrated) attempts by malicious actors to confuse or manipulate people through sharing false information to cause harm (Bradshaw & Howard 2018). In Africa, cases of disinformation have become the norm, especially during elections and civil unrest (see Mare et al. 2019; Maweu 2019; Mare & Matsilele 2020). The mushrooming and circulation of this 'information disorder' has been more pronounced on social media platforms such as WhatsApp, Facebook and Twitter. During the 2017 elections in Kenya, several fake polls were posted on reputable social media pages of established media organisations (Maweu, 2019). One of the widely shared fake polls was assumed to have been set up by the renowned marketing research firm Ipsos Synovate. Most media organisations in Kenya fell for the prank before Ipsos Synovate came out in the open to discredit the poll and the fake website (http://ipsoske.com). The fake opinion poll, released through a legitimate-looking website and circulated to Kenyan media in the name of Ipsos, claimed that the country's incumbent president and Jubilee Party candidate Uhuru Kenyatta had a popularity rating of 47%, ahead of his main opponent and National Super Alliance candidate Raila Odinga, who stood at 44% (Maweu, 2019).

During the 2018 elections in Zimbabwe, there were several incidences of fake news, which was circulated via social media platforms by 'cyber brigades' affiliated to political parties like the Zimbabwe African National Union Patriotic Front (ZANU-PF) and the Movement for Democratic Change Alliance (MDC-A) (Ncube 2019). While ZANU-PF relied on their own social media brigade codenamed '*varakashi*' (local parlance for online thugs), the MDC-A had '*nerrorists*' (a codename for loyalists to the main opposition political leader, derived from his first name, Nelson) who had the role of 'manufacturing' propaganda to discredit opponents. Prior to the announcement of the official results by the Zimbabwe Electoral Commission (ZEC), there was fake news around the manipulation of the voting figures, the hacking of the biometric voting system database and tampering with Excel spreadsheets. For instance, an 'update' circulated on Facebook, WhatsApp and Twitter on 1 August 2018 which read as follows:

> There is now a fresh headache at ZEC command center, BVR (Biometric Voter Registration) statistics, […] international observers' data collection and Civic society results do not tally. Mafigures eZEC aChiwenga ave mahombe kudarika arimuBVR database [ZEC's figures are now exceeding those in the BVR data base]. […] Zimbabweans, […] Chamisa has won. EU observers have the correct statistics as well. Remain peaceful God is in it. Thank you ED for accepting the will of the people.

Interestingly, the authors of the above update claimed to be employees or insiders from ZEC whose role was simply to keep the nation informed on the alleged capture of ZEC by the Vice-President Chiwenga (a former army commander during Mugabe's regime).

In countries that have a long history of lack of trust in the mainstream media, especially the state-controlled media, fake news and disinformation are also intricately connected to popular forms of communication such as music, jokes, humour, subvertisements, cartoons and photoshopped images. As we broadly argue in this book, these informal forms of communication do not spread in thin air nor do they spread in the same way around the world. In the African context, 'fake news' should be understood within the broader and ever-shifting communication ecology made up of formal and informal media as discussed in Chapter 3. Thus, while popular forms of communication provide non literate (and in most cases rural) citizens with the means to engage with news and information (Mare 2020), they also provide an outlet through which false and misleading information is circulated, and audiences cannot always clearly distinguish between which information to trust and which information to simply laugh about (Wasserman 2020). As Eko contends, the 'free-wheeling style' of informal forms of participatory journalism 'is often at odds with 'standard' approaches to journalism or journalistic ethics' (2010, 68). A cartoon that is defensible on grounds of free expression may nevertheless be inappropriate or unwise or miss its target. This has prompted other scholars to submit that we should 'guard against ahistorical approaches' to fake news that overlook its 'critical [...] historical contextualization' (Mare et al. 2019, 7), which points to deeper social issues, anxieties and fears.

Online harassment, hate speech and ethnic stereotypes

One of the most insidious forms of dark participation in the African context is the systemic harassment of female journalists in patriarchal, toxic and polarised political media environments. For instance, journalists like Ferial Haffajee (South Africa, former Editor of *City Press* and the *Mail & Guardian*), Ruvheneko Parirenyatwa (Zimbabwe, radio and TV talk show host), Samantha Musa (Zimbabwe, radio and TV presenter) and Harugumi Mutasa (Zimbabwe, Aljazeera English) have been victims of 'cyber misogyny'. This suggests that offline socio-cultural and political practices are re-enacted digitally in Africa. Thus, online and offline harassment feeds off and into each other in complex but systematic ways. Besides the well-documented structural and cultural violence against women, female journalists are also on the receiving end of symbolic violence on social media platforms like Facebook and Twitter. Hiding behind the cloak of anonymity and fake accounts, cyber misogynists, 'militia', and trolls have resorted to attacking, threatening, smear campaigns, and flooding the social media and email inboxes of female journalists with messages in ways that inadvertently contribute to rising threats against media freedom. The harassment of Sonia Rolley (a former correspondent for *Radio France Internationale* who was based in Kigali, Rwanda, until she was expelled in June 2006) on Twitter for months in 2014 is a good example of how online harassment has become a new way of censoring journalists in Africa (Reporters Without Borders 2016). It was later revealed that the account from which she was being harassed was held by a person who had access to Rwandan President Paul Kagame's social media accounts (Reporters Without Borders 2016). Some female journalists have, however, adopted forms of resistance such as blocking, unfriending, unfollowing and using masked identities and pseudonymous profile names in order to protect themselves from male chauvinists on social media platforms.

Social media accounts administered by mainstream media organisations have also been invaded by unruly publics bent on circulating hate speech, homophobic and xenophobic content, tribal and racist messages. Thus, instead of civil discussions as theorised by Habermas (1989), agonistic and emotional public spheres have become the norm. In Namibia and South Africa, xenophobic messages are circulated through audience participation platforms like letters-to-the-editor, comment sections and social media pages of mainstream media organisations. This chimes with the observation that 'SMS messages and online forums were also on some occasions considered to have been influential in inciting violence' (Willems & Mano 2016, 6). Willems and Mano further observe that 'in the wake of the 2007 elections in Kenya, local language radio stations in particular were accused of hate speech and use of ethnic stereotypes, and were held responsible for the violent incidents that took place in the country' (2016, 6).

Cartoons, humour and other localised informal forms of communication as discussed in Chapter 3 are also caught up in the 'web of toxicity' involving harmful and hateful speech as well as ethnic stereotypes in Africa. For example, in examining the humour circulated by Malawians on social media platforms such as Facebook and WhatsApp, Ngwira and Lipenga (2018, 23) argue that 'the self-denigratory nature that this humour adopts' ultimately works against self-assertion. The humour 'cast[s] Malawians as brutish, idiotic, imbecilic, impoverished, illiterate oafs who delight in, and even celebrate, their own shortcomings'. The danger in such portrayals, which may escape notice amid the laughter, is the perpetuation of stereotypes about a perceived 'common' Malawian. As Ngwira and Lipenga further observe, 'jokes capitalize on perceived eccentricities about a specific group, or certain aspects of their tradition […], or merely emphasize known stereotypes. As a result, [they] can be offensive, and may help to foster antagonism between ethnic groups' (2018, 29). As much as jokes can be a way of coping with everyday hardships (Ngwira & Lipenga 2018) or circumnavigating censorship, where political communication is controlled by a few people, some jokes 'perpetuate dangerous stereotypes that erode people's confidence in themselves and their cultures' (Ngwira & Lipenga 2018, 33). So, while joking about socio-political issues might be a sign of social resilience, they can also point to a sense of shared fears, tensions and anxieties about issues.

The complexities of verifying and moderating social media content

The pervasive nature of misinformation, mal-information and disinformation online exposes journalists to the dangers of distorted information, especially on platforms like Facebook whose very nature as a 'social setting' provides 'no good way for its users to assess whether what they're getting at any given time is [...] intelligent or accurate' (Peters 2011, 155). As one senior reporter at *The Herald* explained: 'People shouldn't read too much into Facebook updates because for most people it's a playground where anything goes. So, if we're to judge people by what they write on their walls, we're heading for disaster [...]'. These concerns led to an ingrained sceptical attitude to Facebook among some senior 'old school' journalists. For example, one veteran editor at *The Zimbabwe Independent* remonstrated thus: 'reporters need to understand that *Facebook is not a Factbook*, it can be a hazardous source of information' (emphasis added). For these cautious journalists, the default approach was to take everything sourced from Facebook with a pinch of salt. This demonstrates a reflective awareness of the potential professional threats embedded in using social media as a journalistic tool. It echoes Berger's (2005, 1) observation that Southern African journalists are far from 'lacking when it comes to critical perspectives with ICTs and global information networks'.

However, despite this critical awareness and scepticism, misinformation and disinformation in African mainstream journalism are closely linked to the challenges of verifying or judging the reliability of information sourced online, particularly on social media platforms, including readers' comments as discussed in Chapter 2. As Singer aptly puts it: 'Online delivery of vast amounts of information creates an even greater need for someone to make sense of it all – someone skilled not only in selecting information but, more importantly, in evaluating it' (1997, 77). From our study, this problem was compounded by senior journalists' poor digital literacy skills and their generally negative attitude towards digital technologies as noted above, which made it easy for copyright infringements to sail through the 'guarded' gates undetected. As one reporter at the *Sunday Mail* explained:

> To be honest, the Internet is posing a real challenge [...] but there is nothing much we can do about it. My boss doesn't know much about the Internet, he is only aware of a few websites he has heard people talk about [...] Half the time he is surprised by the story ideas I glean from the Internet [...].

Under these circumstances, it is difficult for newsrooms to sift out misinformation, mal-information and disinformation, let alone monitor copyright infringements by reporters. This, according to Mare et al. (2019, 6–7) 'points to the culpability of the mainstream media in whipping up 'fake news', an observation often overlooked in African journalism scholarship'. Thus, the varying abilities and attitudes to the use of the internet have serious implications for the ethical dilemmas facing African newsrooms in the era of participatory journalism.

While poor digital skills among senior gatekeepers in the newsrooms broadly related to 'localised' challenges faced by most African digital technology users (because of the pervasive nature of the digital divide), their general attitude to digital technologies also made it difficult for effective gatekeeping strategies to be adopted. This scenario was exacerbated by the lack of clear editorial guidelines and policies, especially in relation to the training of journalists to effectively use the Internet and social media as journalistic tools, as well as keeping abreast with the fast-changing pace of the digital environment. Thus, in most newsrooms, journalists had either been self-taught on the job or relied on skills acquired from friends and colleagues. Commenting on this, a senior desk editor at *The Zimbabwe Independent* stated: 'I have been in this game for the past 14 years, I don't remember ever receiving any form of training on using [digital platforms] as journalistic tools [...] You learn as you go and colleagues chip-in here and there to assist'. This echoes Berger's observation in the mid-2000s that Southern African newsrooms have no formal policies on the training of staff in the use of the Internet, thus resulting in a large proportion of 'peer-to-peer learning and self-teaching in the newsrooms' (2005, 9–10).

The scenario, however, contrasts sharply with developments in the Western world where newsrooms have accepted that they must continuously adapt to the pace of the digital revolution. In a survey of more than 2,000 American journalists and news executives, McLellan and Porter (2007) found that nine in ten newsroom executives agreed that their journalists needed more training. The executives – typically among the most experienced and knowledgeable journalists – also admitted that they needed more training themselves in order to keep abreast of the fast-changing digital environment.

The complexities of verifying online content are directly connected to the lack of structured gate-keeping approaches to managing huge volumes of UGC as discussed in earlier chapters (see Chapters 2 and 5). Although this gap partly hinges on manpower shortages in the newsrooms,[3] some senior editors saw social media platforms, especially Facebook, as a 'playground', not really meriting moderation, albeit useful as a journalistic tool. This contrasted with their view on the UGC on newspaper websites. As the Zimpapers' Group Online Editor explained:

> *Comments on Facebook are often considered inconsequential and social*, but on our websites it's different [...]. It's easy for readers' comments to be associated with our newspapers, which could result in lawsuits. So, we keep a close eye on our newspaper websites instead.

Research in other countries such as South Africa, Kenya and Namibia similarly showed that some media organisations are no longer engaging in the moderation of their social media pages primarily because of the limited human resources running their digital media platforms. Interviews with online editors indicated that, like in the readers' comment sections, they only moderate when a reader has flagged something very offensive and hateful on the site. It is therefore not surprising that a cursory analysis of Facebook and Twitter handles of mainstream media organisations in Zimbabwe, South Africa, Namibia, and Kenya indicated that audiences could post almost anything without any censure from social media editors. This explains the influx of inflammatory comments, especially in instances where individuals hide behind pseudonyms or fake accounts. Thus, unlike in Europe where media organisations have outsourced moderation to companies like eModeration with staff and offices in North America and Australia (Hermida & Thurman 2008), in Africa, as seen in Chapter 2, media organisations have limited financial and human resources to invest in such expensive initiatives.

Some editors were also generally hesitant to consider 'winnowing' (Singer et al. 2011) their social media platforms because of their strategic role in driving traffic to their newspaper websites. Explaining this, AMH's Group Online Editor stated:

We have given our readers free rein on our social media platforms because we want the numbers, they drive to our news websites. As you know, this is important for our advertisers. So, we don't want to be perceived as stifling our loyal online readership.

While the above reluctance to moderate UGC on social media can also be seen as inadvertently providing a corrective balancing act in countries where the press is heavily polarised such as Zimbabwe by giving readers (from across political divides) 'unfettered' space to interact and exchange views, the moderation laxity has opened the flood gates for abuses and extremist political views as discussed above. This demonstrates the challenges faced by newsrooms in encouraging readers to engage with their content while at the same time defending the values of journalism.

'Creative cannibalisation': Recycling news from the newsroom desktop

One of the significant impacts of the Internet and social media on the newsrooms studied in Zimbabwe was apparent in the 'intergroup bias dynamics' (Mudhai 2011) between veteran senior journalists and technologically savvy junior reporters. While the former were more professionally conservative and hardly took part in electronic networking, the latter valued digital technologies, especially the Internet and social media, which they saw as indispensable to their daily routines. These generational tensions embodied the changing face of African journalism in the digital era. Senior and older journalists lamented the dearth of 'shoe leather' reporting[4] as a result of overdependence on web-based content, including UGC, across a range of interactive digital platforms. They worried that the substance of real news was getting lost in what Kawamoto (2003, 26) refers to as 'the technological ornamentation or […] the morass of too much information'. In particular, they deplored the growing culture of laziness in which young journalists spent more time in the newsrooms wedged on their armchairs wading through social media platforms for story ideas than in the field observing directly the events and processes on which they report. As one long-serving senior sports journalist at the *Chronicle* put it:

> The Internet and social media have 'killed' our journalists – they have become armchair reporters. They sit [in the newsroom] and wait for news to come to their desktops. They don't interview anyone; all they do is visit an assortment of [platforms] and generate stories […].

Similarly, a senior news editor at *The Zimbabwe Independent* argued that by enabling journalists to get to data without having to leave the newsroom, the Internet and its associated digital technologies is 'taking away the "human face" of journalism – news stories are now devoid of the "colour" that normally emerges from direct interactions with sources'.

Junior reporters, on the other hand, articulated a contrasting view in support of web-based journalism. As one cub reporter at *The Herald* explained:

> With [social media] on my desk, I don't really have to go out for research; I browse different [platforms] and download stuff right at my desk. That not only saves time, but resources as well […]. Right now I'm working on a story centred on the Durban International Film festival that's taking place in South Africa […]. I'm getting all the information that I want through […] online newspapers. I'm not wasting time at all!

This apparent shift in the traditional practices of newsgathering was further cogently voiced by another junior reporter in a newsroom interview at *The Standard*: 'I'll tell you that in the four stories I've filed today, I've not left my desk […] *that's how efficient we have become!*' (emphasis added). It is thus not surprising that most junior reporters across the newsrooms saw the emphasis on 'shoe leather' reporting by their seniors as counterproductive in a context where 'immediacy' has become the buzzword. One cub reporter vividly expressed his frustration with his seniors by suggesting the need to 'digitise their minds'.

It is interesting, however, to note that despite most senior journalists' professed scepticism in the use of the Internet and social media by their juniors, a few saw the value of the technologies as steeped in the economic context in which the newsrooms operate. They submitted that, to some extent, the Internet, and to a large extent, social media platforms were 'saving the situation' by enabling newsrooms to fulfil their obligation to cover wide-ranging stories even in the context of economic challenges. As one sports editor explained:

> Whereas in the past we could afford to send a reporter to almost every international sporting event for first-hand coverage, nowadays such trips are limited, partly because we are cash-strapped and we know we will get the story on the Internet […] Even our editor will tell you: 'Zimbabwe is playing Zambia in Lusaka next

week, no problem [...], just be on the lookout for what the Zambian newspapers and fans write on the Internet' [...].

While this response reinforces the fact that journalists are increasingly spending more time in the newsrooms, creatively repackaging material already in the public domain, albeit some of it generated by audiences, it is clear that the threats emerging with the appropriation of interactive digital technologies also relate to the intricacies of the economic context in which the newsrooms operate.

The practice of filling space with stale or pre-packaged material was also particularly evident in the use of the email – one of the most widely used interactive technologies of the Internet era in all the newsrooms studied. While many young reporters glorified the speed, flexibility and efficiency of email, a number of senior journalists were wary of using the technology as a journalistic tool. The senior reporters described the technology as less transparent and exposing journalists to the risk of unreliable sources as well as curtailing initiative by promoting a culture of '*sedentary journalism*'. Further criticising the practice of generating stories from emails, some senior reporters argued that engaging with sources through email 'eliminates the candour, spontaneity and natural dialogue, [...] and the essential context to a story'. The legitimacy of these concerns was illustrated in the extract below from a newsroom interview with a young email enthusiast at *The Herald*:

REPORTER: Look, you see this email? It's from the Zimbabwe Tourism Authority; they sent it yesterday [...] If you look in today's paper you will see the story, I generated from this. [he picks up a copy of the day's paper on his desk and leafs through it to show me the story he had written based on the email].
INTERVIEWER: So, you did this story based on the email you have just shown me?
REPORTER: Yes, as you see, they sent me this bit, it's about four paragraphs and I blew it up (sic) into the story you see in that newspaper. I simply added context and 'life' to the email [...] These are my regular sources; they are constantly informing me about the latest developments [...] and from their emails I write stories [...].

This extract shows how the appropriation of email militates against the journalistic ideal of original reportage by promoting what former BBC journalist Waseem Zakir famously branded as 'churnalism' – the practice of reengineering already existing material and turning it into news reports (Harcup 2008). Thus, while it is generally argued that the appropriation of interactive digital technologies reflects national contexts, there are many ways in which emerging participatory practices in African journalism 'borrow from and build on global developments' (Mudhai 2011, 674), and as elsewhere, these developments are overturning the basics of journalism.

'Elite news accessing': Shifting news access and sourcing routines

The growing practice of newsroom-bound journalism discussed above, in which reporters barely leave the newsroom for first-hand encounters with their sources has marked implications on news access and sourcing routines in Africa. From our observations and interviews in this study, it was clear that overdependence on the Internet and its associated digital technologies by young reporters was promoting an 'elitist news sourcing culture' of sorts, which favours sections of society with access and the means to appropriate digital technologies in ways that facilitate the projection of a visibility that catches the attention of journalists who are under constant deadline pressure.

Although the mainstream press has always been criticised for its 'elitist' posturing, overdependence on interactive digital technologies in contexts characterised by sharp disparities in access to technologies (as is the case in most sub-Saharan African countries) cements relations between elite forces and newsmakers thus partly influencing who gets on the news. The technologies therefore structure routine entry into news in such a way that only sources with the infrastructure that guarantees a reliable and steady supply of the raw materials of news are privileged in the news. This 'over-accessing to the media' (Hall et al. 1978, 58) by a few privileged and techno-savvy individuals inadvertently 'annihilates' those existing on the margins of digital platforms, thus underlining the fact that technology is 'not a neutral agent', rather it reinforces 'traditional norms as much as to enact change' (Robinson 2011, 1135).

The appropriation of social media platforms, Facebook in particular, by entertainment reporters provides a good example of the impact of digital technologies on news access and sourcing (see Chapter 3). A regular observation of Web browsers in some of the newsrooms revealed that entertainment reporters invested more time on Facebook than their colleagues in other news beats, and this tended to limit the scope of their story ideas as well as the voices cited in the stories. As one veteran entertainment journalist explained:

the problem with journalists spending more time lurking on famous people's Facebook profiles is that it slants their stories towards the more affluent and educated [...]. Journalists miss a lot of good ideas outside these networks [...]. *There are many entertainers [in this country] who are semi-literate and can't operate a computer, let alone [post content on social media].*

(emphasis added)

This response highlights how reliance on web-based interactive digital technologies for story ideas tends to narrow the perspective of reporters, marginalising potential story ideas from sources that are not digitally connected. This is particularly the case in contexts of material depriva-tion where ordinary citizens have limited *access* to digital technologies – at least to the extent of shaping and influencing news content, thanks to the social impact of the 'digital divide', which includes '(digital) skills or competencies' (van Dijk 2006, 224). Thus, while digital technologies bring about journalistic opportunities, they can also marginalise large populations who do not have access. Access to social media and other digital platforms promotes new hierarchies where a small tech-savvy elite gain influence at the expense of the majority. In the context of enter-tainment reporting, individuals who actively participate on social media become the 'primary definers' (Hall et al. 1978, 61) of news. They com-mand the discursive field and set the agenda for issues covered by entertainment reporters much to the annihilation of potential sources without the means or knowledge to effectively deploy and appropriate the Internet and its associated technologies. In this sense, it could be argued that in selected African newsrooms, interactive digital technolo-gies are far from broadening or democratising news production, rather they are narrowing the perspectives of reporters, particularly where face-to-face contact with sources is dispensed with.

In addition to the above, despite 'perceptions that, in Africa, time is not as important as it is in the developed world' (Mudhai, 2011, 678), the practical pressures of constantly working against the clock (and the need to meet required story quotas), which have intensified with the era of partici-patory journalism, also appear to reinforce the over-accessing of news by those with sustained means to supply stories. From newsroom observations and interviews, it was clear that when under deadline pressure, the Internet and social media platforms were almost always the default fall-back for journalists. As one political reporter at *The Herald* explained:

You have to get news as quickly as possible [...] so obviously inaccessible areas will have very little news access [...]. It's even worse if they are not connected to the latest technologies like [social media]. I might drive to the areas but the problem is that my competitors will be moving on with the latest stories [...].

Thus, as information becomes readily available on various interactive platforms, reporters are fixed on 'scooping' rather than ensuring that the story is balanced.

While elite news access cannot be attributed solely to journalists' overreliance on interactive digital technologies, particularly social media, the significance of this 'crisis' in most African newsrooms, however, needs to be interpreted in the context of the structural complexities of *connectivity* and *access*, which place elite news sources at a vantage point to define and pontificate what is newsworthy.

It is important, however, to note that this biasing of news in African newsrooms is not down to technology alone but to the 'convergence of many forces that [are] contingent upon local circumstances' (Fenton, 2010, 5), including the dynamics of gender. Thus, although women are part of the emerging culture of participatory journalism in Africa, men dominate as civic instigators and contributors by projecting the loudest voices online, which is generally reflective of the patriarchal nature of news consumption and political participation on the continent (Mare 2016). Besides gender, age, race, ethnicity, geographical location (mostly urbanites and those in the disapora), level of education and class are key factors in shaping the nature of digital participation (and visibility) in Africa. For example, Africans living in the diaspora have tended to dominate online conversations on socio-political issues affecting their home countries more than those domiciled in the homeland because of their access to faster, cheaper and reliable Internet. Reflecting on the South African context, Wasserman (2018) argues that the continued asymmetry of power in the social domain and the political economy of digital media platforms allow middle class, white voices to be heard more often than those of marginalised groups.

While it is indeed reductionist to attribute 'elite news accessing' (Mabweazara 2013, 144) to interactive digital technologies alone, it seems clear from the discussion above that overreliance on social media places individuals who wield 'social hegemony' (Schudson 2000, 184) in an advantageous position in terms of defining what makes news. Collectively, these dynamics reinforce previous studies which have indicated that communication on the web is characterised by a 'power law distribution' in which a tiny minority of Internet users produces the content consumed by the majority. The foregoing contextual factors result in journalistic subjectivities that have placed notions of 'objectivity and impartiality, the holy grail of professional journalism, under scrutiny' (Fenton 2010, 8).

Diminishing spatial boundaries and the invasion of personal privacy

In reflecting on the professional challenges emerging with the use of social media, a number of journalists underlined the dilemmas they faced in negotiating the platforms' tendency to blur the line between the *professional* and the personal *subjective individual*. They spoke about the difficulties they faced in publicly expressing their personal opinions on controversial issues generated on Facebook and Twitter. In one revealing case in 2014, a journalist at *The Daily Monitor* in Uganda was forced by the newspaper's management to publicly apologise for posting blistering comments about Rwandan President Paul Kagame on his personal Facebook page following the murder of former Rwandan intelligence chief, Patrick Karegeya, in South Africa (Reporters Without Borders 2016). This incident reinforces the dilemmas faced by journalists in negotiating the blurring lines between the *professional* and the personal *subjective individual* on social media.

Journalists in Zimbabwe described how this dilemma put them in the spotlight and subjected them to scathing criticisms from their employers as well as the public, precisely because of the general expectation that journalists should maintain a public deportment that does not put their impartiality into question. One senior news reporter at *The Zimbabwe Independent* lucidly explained this point:

> Although, like anybody else, I'm tickled and provoked by some of the issues raised by my friends on Facebook, *I deliberately avoid commenting on those issues I think would put me on a tight spot. I try not to expose my personal convictions, in case I'm generally perceived as impartial and lacking objectivity in my work.*
>
> (emphasis added)

The 'self-censorship' highlighted in the extract above points to the challenges journalists face in negotiating the tensions between private life and work on social media. Facebook in particular is seen as intruding into aspects of their private life 'leading to a blurring of the distinction between private and professional life' (Mabweazara 2013, 146). Most journalists expressed their frustration at how this implicitly stifled their personal freedom. As one junior sports reporter explained:

You will understand that as long as you are in formal employment the voice on your Facebook wall will always be linked to your employer [...]. Personally, I don't know how many times I've been asked why I write so passionately about Dynamos Football Club on my Facebook profile by my desk editor [...]. It's worrying.

These concerns point to the broader crisis facing journalism in the era of digital technologies, which has seen the right to personal privacy and space coming under unprecedented threat.

Linked to the challenges of navigating personal privacy are ethical questions associated with journalists using material posted on individuals' Facebook profiles in news stories without their consent or knowledge. Journalists tend to lurk on prominent personalities' profiles for story ideas, completely disregarding issues of privacy. When probed about this ethical dilemma a number of reporters pointed to the fine line between privacy and public life on social media. One entertainment reporter at *The Standard* explained thus: 'If an artist posts something of interest on their Facebook profile, I would definitely use it because [...] It's already "public knowledge" and, irrefutably, they are the main source of that comment'. This state of affairs, as Duff (2008) puts it, is another clear manifestation of the controversy surrounding privacy in the digital era. It illustrates 'the normative crisis of the information society' (Duff 2008), which has seen the right to personal privacy and space coming under unprecedented threat.

The absence of codified policy guidelines on how journalists should use or conduct themselves on social media platforms appeared to exacerbate the ethical challenges across the news organisations studied. While Zimpapers has a detailed set of what it calls 'community rules and guidelines' for its web-content users (see Chapter 2), it does not specifically address how its staffers should use social media as a journalistic tool. This scenario finds similarity in other African newsrooms. Writing about the virtual lack of social media policies in Zambian newsrooms, Mambwe observes that '[d]espite acknowledging the value that social media play, the editors were sceptical on whether the impact that has been observed is significant enough to warrant shifts in policy' (Mambwe 2019, 36).

Navigating and managing the tensions between private and professional lives is also a serious challenge for Western media institutions, including big newspapers. However, most news organisations in advanced economies have developed clear policies or guidelines for their staffers. For example, as early as September 2009, *The Washington Post* had published social media guidelines, which outlined how its journalists should conduct themselves on social media as well as the 'potential hazards' associated with using the technologies.[5] The policy makes it clear that journalists can be fired if their social media activities 'adversely affects *The Post*'s customers, advertisers, subscribers, vendors, suppliers or partners' (Beaujon 2019). Similarly, in a memo to journalists in 2012, the Associate Managing Editor for standards at *The New York Times*, Philip Corbett, reminded journalists that the rapid expansion of social media presents some new challenges:

> As we continue to expand our efforts in social media, here's a reminder. [...] *you are a Times journalist, and your online behavior should be appropriate for a Times journalist. Readers will inevitably associate anything you post on social media with The Times. [...] Take care that nothing you say online will undercut your credibility as a journalist.*
>
> (Sullivan 2012, emphasis added)

Likewise, *The Los Angeles Times*' social media policy boldly warns journalists as follows: 'Assume that your professional life and your personal life merge online regardless of your care in separating them. Don't write or post anything that would embarrass the LAT or compromise your ability to do your job'.[6]

Although developments in AI offer some intriguing possibilities for tackling editorial gaps and limitations in African news media, they also have the potential to entrench old normative dilemmas as well as creating new ones. These warrant close attention as we discuss in the next section.

Automated dilemmas and potential ethical challenges

Journalistic decision making, albeit in the moderation of readers' comments, 'often involves ethical choices based on long-held values, guided by [established] editorial standards' (Chadwick 2018). However, technological actants such as algorithms, chatbots and other communicative agents do not have the sense of accountability that human beings wield. Equally, given that algorithms are programmed by humans who have inherent biases, they have a potential to mislead. In the words of Noble, '[w]hile we often think of terms such as "big data" and "algorithms" as being benign, neutral, or objective' (Noble 2018, 1–2), they are anything but neutral. People who programme these technologies in journalistic contexts hold all types of values, which shape and constrain participatory practices and forms of audience engagement. It for this reason that Chadwick (2018) argues that '[s]ome

AI-processed data can be tainted with ethnic, gender or other types of bias because of assumptions that humans built in, consciously or otherwise'. Thus, when it comes to automated moderation discussed in Chapter 5, questions around the ability of machines to make ethical decisions and the kind of values that undergird algorithmic decision making emerge. It is precisely for these reasons that journalists will always need to cross-check and verify algorithmic outcomes (Chadwick 2018).

It is important, however, to note that automated technology can also be used to propagate and circulate misinformation, disinformation and hate speech, especially in countries with high levels of political and social instability such as Zimbabwe. While user comment sections are well-known 'breeding grounds' for hate speech and disinformation, AI-generated 'deep fakes', or what some refer to as 'disinformation on steroids' are 'highly realistic and difficult-to-detect' (Chesney & Citron 2018) forms of disinformation deployed, especially during critical moments like elections (see Maweu 2019). Elections in countries like Zimbabwe, South Africa, Kenya and Nigeria have been known to be marred by the indiscriminate sharing of fake news and cyber-propaganda generated by political parties through deploying 'cyber troops' (Mare & Matsilele 2020).

Writing about the 2007 Kenyan elections, Maweu (2019, 62) observes that the results of the election were 'largely dismissed as "fake computer-generated results" due to the alleged cyber propaganda and the extensive spread of disinformation' engineered by 'Cambridge Analytica, a British data mining firm that offered services on influencing voter behaviour to the presidential candidate, Uhuru Kenyatta while 'smearing the image of his main rival, Raila Odinga, behind the scenes'.[7] Maweu (2019, 65) notes that 'bots made up the highest share of influencers' in the 'elections, accounting for 26% of all influential users who took part in Twitter conversations'.

While fake news and disinformation are not new in Africa (see Mare et al. 2019), the 'automation turn' takes these established social problems to a whole new level because of the heightened 'capacity to create hyper realistic, [and] difficult-to-debunk fake [...] content' (Chesney & Citron 2018). The participatory platforms explored in this book, especially social media, are all well-suited for the spread of 'hyper realistic' misleading information. This has potentially catastrophic consequences in sub-Saharan Africa where digital literacy levels that can debunk these clandestine automated activities are low relative to countries in the developed North. 'Deep fakes' can thus be used to emphasise extant ethnic and religious divisions, and 'to attack nascent democratic institutions' (Besaw & Filitz 2019).

One of the concerns emerging with the appropriation of AI in Africa is the relegation of carefully thought-out journalistic decision making to the back burner in favour of decisions underpinned by computational data. The increasing use of editorial metrics to shape decisions on what content to deliver to readers directly implicates questions of 'journalistic transparency'. Equally, it is not always obvious what personal data is being collected to inform editorial processes, especially for the ordinary reader. However, as Ronderos (2019) contends, if news organisations 'want to be different from the manipulators and demagogues who secretly collect data for use as a commercial or political weapon', they should explain to their readers how they are using automation in editorial processes. This is particularly important in Africa where distrust in the news media and state surveillance is not only pervasive but intricately connected to the polarised political environments which obtain in most countries (see Parks & Mukherjee 2017).

Although automated audience data collection allows news organisations to cater to their audiences' taste, 'the choice to be transparent often means sacrificing other benefits such as profit and scalability' (Renner 2017), which most news organisations are not always willing to do. For this reason, audience metrics have also been used by some media organisations to churn out clickbait headlines, especially on social media, with the intention of driving traffic to their websites. It has also seen the proliferation of sensationalised content intended to attract more clicks, views and shares.

In contexts already grappling with entrenched inequalities of access, low digital literacy levels and a general lack of understanding of how power is expressed through technology, the outsourcing of editorial decision making to machines has dire implications. As Noble (2018, 1) puts it, the 'digital decisions' reinforce existing 'oppressive social relationships', power and privilege. In most African countries, the negative impact of these deeply insidious technologies is widely left unquestioned due to low digital literacy levels and the inability to understand the technical processes underpinning AI in most newsrooms, even for seasoned journalists. This inability to discern exactly what 'machines' are doing behind the scenes is thus problematic for journalists (and inevitably for audiences). It also partly explains the lack of transparency by news organisations on how exactly they deploy automated tools to moderate readers' comments, fact-check news or harness audience metrics. While the lack of transparency in African news media is not necessarily new (see Mabweazara 2018), the 'underground' nature of AI reinforces this established culture.

Thus, while participatory practices associated with AI are often blissfully conceived as neutral, they are far from it and in reality are infused with particular agendas (Kwet 2019). The programming of algorithms to track and supply more of what users are looking for on digital media based on their location, past behaviours etc., resulting in users becoming 'more ensconced' in filter bubbles and encountering fewer and fewer alternative views (Markham 2017, 11) is one classic example of how algorithms are infused with 'hidden agendas'. It also points to another catastrophic consequence of the lack of transparency in the deployment of automated technology. The lack of transparency in particular has significant implications in shaping participatory practices 'because it cuts [users/readers] off from people with different views and interests [and] seriously undermines public deliberation' (Markham 2017, 11). This is a major concern in Africa as the discreet algorithms tend to feed readers with news they want to see, rather than a balanced, bipartisan diet. In the end, while it is broadly true that the use of AI reinvigorates journalism as never before (Chadwick 2018), it is also true that this ushers in new challenges.

The above threats and dilemmas have led to calls for the inspection of algorithms and the designing of ethical news bots as well as effective moderation practices (see Chapters 1 and 4). Unfortunately, the highly uneven distribution of resources and knowledge required to implement AI techniques render decision making about which applications to adopt and which ones to avoid difficult. Similarly, differences in attitudes to technology, especially between the younger generation and old school journalists, also directly influence automated participatory practices. There are no silver bullet solutions; however, where resources permit, a robust digital literacy programme within news organisations is necessary.

Conclusion

This chapter has provided an overview of the normative and ethical dilemmas emerging with participatory journalism in Africa. It reinforces the fact that the era of participatory journalism is redefining the means by which journalists engage with their readers as well as how readers relate and respond to news content. We have established that interactive digital technologies are not only redefining the professional values, norms and ideals of journalism but also reshaping everyday routines as well as influencing the strategic direction and practice of journalism in Africa. With these developments, traditional ethical concerns such as the proliferation of hate speech and the so-called 'fake news' as well as the invasion of personal privacy have taken on new meanings.

While some of these transformations are global, the chapter also highlights the contingent nature of the crises facing African journalism in the era of *participatory journalism*. As Campbell contends: '[t]he crises of journalism in many parts of the developing world are significantly more overt and pressing' (2004, 256), and in many ways different from the crises facing journalism in developed countries. Thus, interactive and participatory technologies in a context characterised by disproportionate access to digital technologies promotes a shrinking diversity of voices in the news. These challenges are exacerbated by the absence of policy frameworks on the appropriation of digital technologies in newsrooms as well as the lack of accountability and a sense of responsibility among journalists themselves. The adoption and appropriation of AI in particular adds a new layer to these challenges, including the lack of transparency in algorithmic decision making.

In general, the challenges discussed above call for a critical reflection on the substance of journalism in the context of a technological revolution that has its own contradictions in order to safeguard the traditional normative values and standards of journalism, as well as the integrity and respect for personal privacy, all of which appear to be under undue threat in the era of participatory journalism. Critical thinking still needs to explore and assess the value that should be attached to participatory and interactive cultures, and how exactly they should be integrated into everyday journalistic practices. Further, journalists clearly require new skills and training on a range of techniques surrounding participatory UGC and social media, as well as judgment about when and how to use information sourced from these interactive platforms.

Notes

1 James Curran sums up these technological attributes as 'interactivity, global reach, cheapness, speed, networking facility, storage capacity and alleged uncontrollability' (2016, 2).
2 The *information superhighway* was a popular term used throughout the 1990s to refer to digital communication systems, especially the Internet.
3 For example, Zimpapers' Group Online Editor was responsible for single-handedly managing content from all the newspapers' interactive platforms (i.e. updating and editing all the newspapers' websites as well as populating and monitoring various social media platforms across all newspapers).
4 'Shoe leather' reporting refers to 'news-gathering when the journalist is on the scene [...] out in the field observing directly the events and processes on which they report' (Pavlik 2000, 229).

5 *Washington Post*'s Social Media Policy. Retrieved from: https://insidesocialm
   edia.com/social-media-policies/washington-posts-social-media-policy/ [acces-
   sed 20 June 2020].
6 'Los Angeles Times Social Media Guidelines'. Retrieved from: https://mem
   bers.newsleaders.org/resources-ethics-lasocial [accessed 20 June 2020].
7 Although related firms still exist, Cambridge Analytica ceased operating in
   2018 in the wake of a data scandal involving Facebook.

6   Participation, pitfalls, predicaments and 'new' normative directions

Concluding reflections

This book has offered an African perspective on how news organisations are embracing digital participatory practices as part of their everyday news production, dissemination and audience engagement practices. Drawing on empirical evidence from sub-Saharan Africa, we have examined how developments in interactive digital technologies are redefining traditional journalistic cultures, culminating in practices that are transforming journalism both structurally in terms of established routines and normatively in terms of the resulting professional and ethical dilemmas. Journalists and audiences across sub-Saharan Africa are embracing a wide-range of digital participatory practices that, as we have seen, are anchored in three intricately connected variants of participatory journalism, namely: 1) practices rooted in *generic technological affordances* of interactive digital technologies; 2) *automated participatory practices*; and 3) *context-specific participatory practices and cultures* in which ordinary citizens wield more agency in shaping participatory practices. The three variants constitute what can be interpreted as a complex ecology of participatory journalism in Africa, although they certainly find similarity in other regions of the economically developing world.

We have broadly adopted a social constructivist approach, which emphasises the social shaping and 'interpretive flexibility' of technology – particularly how technologies should be understood as continuous with and embedded in the social realities and dynamics in which they are deployed and appropriated (Bijker 1995). This theoretical orientation challenges the 'technicist' view that in Africa, interactive digital platforms are the *sine qua non* spaces for democratic participation, a view that disregards digital literacy levels and the general impact of the digital divide. Thus, rather than merely foregrounding and celebrating user-participatory practices in African journalism, we also highlight the elite-centric nature of participation on digital platforms as well as a range of ethical and normative pitfalls. We point to some of the manipulations and hidden structural controls to participation and engagement in which ordinary citizens unknowingly respond to and engage with automated cues facilitated by AI, chatbots and algorithms. When examining participatory journalism, we therefore need to consider it in context by acknowledging the fact that although it is underpinned by 'generic technological affordances' and 'automated participatory practices', as noted above, it inevitably assumes localised forms or *context-specific participatory practices and cultures* that are coloured by the material and social circumstances in which it emerges.

Some key observations

In examining how sub-Saharan African journalists are handling the 'new' digitised context in which strangers contribute and respond directly to something they alone once controlled, we broadly observe that although the newsrooms are still largely adjusting to the practice of interactivity and the permeation of readers' voices into their territory, the developments are influencing and challenging newsroom practices in ways that point to an ecological reconfiguration of the established news culture. Readers' comment forums, for example, are providing a useful extra layer of functionality that complements existing practices through providing story ideas, engendering public debate as well as holding journalists to account by exposing poor journalistic practice. This form of 'participatory journalism' also provides an opportunity for readers to interact with each other and express agreement or disagreement with other comments. While there are ad hoc efforts towards content moderation, there is still a lack of clear gatekeeping strategies in most news organisations (see Chapter 2), and this has opened floodgates of abuse as well as the circulation of extremist views that pose serious threats to the core values of news and the normative ideals of traditional journalism.

Similarly, the integration of social media platforms across newsrooms is redefining the means by which journalists engage with their audiences as well as how audiences relate and respond to the news content. The interactive and participatory cultures emerging on platforms such as Facebook and Twitter are turning newsrooms into what Singer et al. have termed an 'open, ongoing' collaborative 'social experiment' (2011, 1) that gives readers unprecedented access to the social production and reception of news. Equally, but on a different level, the era of AI as it manifests through the strategic deployment of chatbots and algorithms by newsrooms has ushered in a new level of deeply insidious automated participatory practices that are unsettling established forms of news media audience participation and engagement. Participatory cultures influenced by AI agents on social media platforms such as Facebook and Twitter are presenting serious challenges in terms of the authenticity and 'organic nature' of user engagement, especially in the light of extant questions on digital literacy levels and the general impact of the 'digital divide' on the African continent. Collectively, these developments are transforming established traditional newsmaking practices and cultures in ways that still require further and ongoing scrutiny, beyond what we have covered in this book.

In some contexts, mainstream media organisations have recruited content moderators and social media experts to moderate, respond to, analyse and even attempt to monetise the large volumes of data emerging from developing cultures of user participatory practices. The measurement of user engagement and participatory practices using editorial metrics has also significantly altered news production and distribution patterns (see Moyo, D. et al. 2019). What we learn from this is that while newsrooms are still broadly adjusting to the influx of readers' voices in their territory, the voices are increasingly shaping and contributing to the dynamics of newsmaking in ways that point to an emerging ecological reconfiguration and recasting of dimensions of news production and consumption.

The study has also noted that besides popular communication on newspaper websites, some of the participatory forms of journalism we have identifed have taken the form of *SMS text messages to the Editor* and *social media comments* because of the relative affordability of these technologies. In countries like Zimbabwe, social media bundles offered by mobile network providers such as Econet and NetOne have promoted particular bias towards the use of social media platforms like WhatsApp, Facebook and Twitter. In Zimbabwe, as elsewhere in Africa, mobile phone calls are generally expensive when compared to the use of social media bundles. This partly explains why most newspapers, radio stations and television stations have embedded social media platforms into their audience engagement strategies.

As the study has shown, in order to understand participatory journalism in Africa, there is a need to critically analyse the broader structural aspects of African media, their markets and the political economy of journalism on the continent. These and other structural circumstances shape and constrain the ways in which news organisations have adapted to new ways of directly relating and engaging with their audiences, and attempts to exploit artificial intelligence, chatbots and algorithms. Thus, the political economy of participatory journalism in Africa requires a more nuanced analysis as it speaks to both established and teething problems that potentially undermine the 'democratic' and participatory potential of digital technologies. Issues like accessibility, affordability, speed and availability of the Internet are increasingly shaping the nature and scope of participatory journalism, especially in contexts where 'digital authoritarianism' in the form of Internet shutdowns and slowdowns and digital surveillance are threatening access to information, freedom of speech and 'assembly' in the digital arena. Thus, while the architecture and arena of audience participation has been broadened by interactive digital technologies, this book underscores the importance of recognising the existence of participatory inequalities.

The pitfalls and dark side of participation: Hate speech, misogyny and the illusion of free participation

As discussed in Chapter 5, the 'participatory turn' has also spawned the 'dark side' (Quandt 2018) of participation through practices such as the online harassment of female journalists in toxic patriarchal and polarised political media environments. Besides being victims of structural and cultural violence, female journalists have been on the receiving end of 'cultural and symbolic violence' on social media platforms like Facebook, Twitter and WhatsApp. As we have observed, hiding behind the clock of anonymity and fake accounts, cyber-misogynists, bots, trolls and cyber-militia have been enlisted, especially in moments of political upheaval, to attack, threaten or engage in smear campaigns through flooding social media and email inboxes with messages. This has inadvertently contributed to threats against media freedom and suggests that digital media platforms can be used in ways that replicate offline socio-cultural and political practices. The key observation here is that online spaces amplify existing socio-political and cultural practices.

The dark side of participation also manifests itself through the circulation of hate speech, xenophobic, misogynistic and tribal messages, especially in polarised contexts like Zimbabwe, Malawi, Namibia, South Africa and Kenya. We have also highlighted the mushrooming of online echo chambers along similar lines, and the recruitment and deployment of cyber-trolls and bots. Similarly, mass production and dissemination of disinformation and cyber-propaganda are rife, particularly in moments of crisis and political tension.

It is important, however, to note that depending on the socio-political context, readers' comment sections as *invited spaces of participation* have engendered both democratic and authoritarian deliberation. Whereas in countries like Kenya and South Africa, readers' comments have nurtured a climate of democratic deliberation, in more restrictive countries like eSwatini and Zimbabwe, comment spaces have normalised the culture of *'authoritarian deliberation'* (He 2006) which places structural limitations upon open public discussion and debate. In authoritarian countries the fear of overstepping boundaries of public speech shapes the nature and content of online conversations and there are a variety of reasons why offline conversations may not be reproduced online. These include feelings of indifference, disillusionment or apathy, or simply not wanting to be seen by others as 'being political'. Thus, the use of readers' comment sections and social media platforms in news production and engagement is influenced by the broader political and cultural context, and prevailing surveillance practices and fears. The fear of communication surveillance, in particular, turns interactive media, especially social media, into a disempowering space in authoritarian contexts (Mare 2016). This explains why in authoritarian countries readers' comments, especially on public/state-controlled media websites and social media platforms, are predominantly characterised by a 'spiral of silence' as people are wary of state digital surveillance activities. However, as we have shown in Chapter 3, in order to circumvent these structural impediments, users in sub-Saharan African countries have resorted to the use of *oblique voices* by memifying politics through jokes, gossip, subvertisements, cartoons and other avenues of popular communication when commenting on or engaging with mainstream media content online (Mare 2020).

Thus, readers' comment sections, interactive websites and social media platforms can be viewed as 'sites of power struggles' where, for example, content moderators, state-surveillance agents, corporate forces and platform-specific code coalesce to foster subtle but powerful 'gatekeeping' practices that nurture what can be referred to as 'staged authenticity' in participatory journalism. These 'masked' gatekeeping practices therefore challenge claims by techno-optimists that digital interactive platforms are the *sine qua non* spaces for symmetrical and democratic participation in the digital agora.

Beyond the rhetoric and smokescreen of participatory journalism: Who participates, when, why, how and under what conditions?

It is important to note that while *invited spaces of participation* on news websites and social media platforms have allowed users to engage directly with media content, not everyone is able to participate, especially in terms of contributing to the convivial online discussions. The various conceptions of participation explored in this book allow us to closely examine the nature of participatory practices in media production contexts as well as the influence of elite interests that may manifest behind the *rhetoric of participatory journalism*. For example, because of their architectural design, social media platforms reinvigorate what Fraser (1990, 72) refers to as '*strong publics*', which are spaces of institutionalised deliberation whose discourse encompasses both opinion formation and decision-making. This is synonymous with *active participants* of participatory journalism. On the other hand, readers' comment sections only provide space for users to engage in '*permitted reactive participation*' (Olsson & Svensson 2012) and hence fall within what Carpentier (2011) calls the '*minimalist forms of participation*' which is 'characterized by [...] strong power imbalances between the actors' (2011, 32). This is partly because online editors 'set the frames for the content and control infrastructure as well as the production process' (Jönsson & Örnebring 2011, 140).

It can therefore be argued that social media platforms like Facebook, Twitter, YouTube and WhatsApp foster what Jönsson and Örnebring (2011) describe as an '*interactive illusion*'. This is primarily because the participatory nature of these spaces is significantly limited or skewed towards those with quality access and the ability to effectively use the platforms, and as such, terms like 'mediated quasi-interaction' (Thompson 2020, 10) are more appropriate descriptors. This corroborates the view that top-down goal-oriented participation models impose institutional barriers over audiences thereby inhibiting other processes that promote empowerment and freedom. In short, participation in practice is not often *participatory, bottom-up* and *open* (Carpentier 2011). Rather, as we have argued, it maintains existing power relationships, albeit masking this power behind the rhetoric and techniques of participation. Thus, claims to full participation on readers' comment sections and social media platforms all too often turn out to be situations in which only the voices and versions of the vocal and privileged few are raised and heard (Cornwall 2002). As Gaventa (2006) posits, without a critical engagement with multiple sources of power inequalities, it is likely that spaces of participatory journalism may further entrench power inequalities. These dynamics are at the very core of the normative dilemmas facing participatory journalism in Africa as discussed in Chapter 5.

One of the main observations we have made in this book is that *participation engendered by generic technological affordances* often mirrors offline participatory dynamics. This reinforces questions around the notion of 'access' to digital technologies, which, as we have seen, does not automatically translate into participation. In the words of Carpentier (2011, 31), 'access and interaction remain important conditions of the possibility of participation, but they cannot be equated with participation'. Similar views have been expressed by scholars who argue that the same people who have social, cultural, or economic capital in offline spaces also exert their influence in online spaces (see Mare 2016). In the context of news production in Africa, as seen in Chapters 2 and 5, these become the 'primary definers' of news (Hall et al. 1978). This confirms Fraser's (1990) view that participatory privileges are enjoyed by members of dominant social groups. Thus, achieving participatory parity on social media platforms and readers' comment sections is only possible if underlying economic, cultural and status inequalities are first addressed.

Language also influences participatory dynamics on readers' comment sections and social media platforms. There are two kinds of language on invited and invented spaces of participation: the *language of the platform* (structured by code and algorithms) as well as the *language of users* (vernacular, official and slang etc.) (Mare 2016). The jettisoning of the *language of the platform* in favour of the *language of users* signifies the creative tempering with the structure put in place by designers and the manifestation of human agency through the use of vernacular language and code switching online (Mare 2016). The use of one particular language over another should, however, not be trivialised. It can be exclusionary to those who do not share the same language by those who have the *cultural* and *linguistic capital* to engage in the English-dominated conversations. Thus, the dominance of English language on digital platforms remains a fault-line which hampers the realisation of full participatory journalism in Africa.

Who controls the gate? The dynamics of gatekeeping

Contrary to cyber-optimistic accounts about the end of gatekeeping in the digital age, we have broadly argued that content moderation or digital gatekeeping remains very important as it was in the analogue era. Although a thorn in the flesh for online editors, gatekeeping is used to prevent or retrospectively remove 'objectionable' material from sites in line with formal and informal standards of acceptable use. In the context of news websites, online editors in some newsrooms have become active curators of UGC on comment sections instead of providing a neutral and open space. They have 'largely sought to maintain their professional control, acting cautiously when it comes to enabling citizens to participate in news production processes via their proprietary platforms' (Westlund & Murschetz 2019, 59).

As discussed in Chapter 2, online editors in various newsrooms highlighted that they draw on a cocktail of strategies albeit inconsistently to restrict content and participation on their readers' comment sections and social media platforms. The strategies included *censoring by deletion, censoring by hiding*, and *censoring by blocking* (see Figure 2.1). *Censoring by deletion* points to the practice of removing content which is considered unpalatable from a page or discussion thread. This means that content which has been deleted can no longer be seen by other participants on the social media platform or comment section. *Censoring by hiding* refers to the practice of hiding posts deemed as sowing discord from the wall or discussion thread instead of an outright banishment from the forum. This frames the possibilities for engagement, circumscribing what can be said and what cannot by defining the contours of what is up for discussion and shunting other considerations out of the frame (Cornwall 2002). *Censoring by blocking* denotes the outright banning of a participant from a page or group in cases of repeated or extreme violation of the 'silent' norms and guidelines. These 'gatekeeping' dynamics are complicated by the subtle but deeply insidious forms of control deployed by platform companies like Facebook, relying on algorithms and AI as well as human fact checkers to guide 'individual behaviour and maintain collective norms' (Lackatt 2005, 1).

Collectively, the approaches limit the potential for competing views and the free flow of alternative ideas since some voices are either silenced or totally banished from entering the spaces of participation. Thus, without necessarily denying the participatory potential of readers' comments, social media platforms and interactive websites, this book acknowledges 'the limitations of and constraints to these participative and democratic potentials' (Cammaerts 2008, 360). In other words, the dynamics of participation on various platforms will vary 'according to who creates [and manages] the space [...], and therefore, whose rules of the game are used to determine who enters the space, and how they behave once they do' (Gaventa 2006, 60).

Participatory journalism as 'the new normative': Some final thoughts

From the above, it is clear that participatory journalism in Africa is inflected by 'impediments to participatory parity' (Fraser 1990, 79). The barriers to equal participation include the cost of accessing the

Internet (and associated digital technologies); low digital literacy skills; the hidden structural impediments of digital technologies; fear of communication surveillance; and the lack of the required linguistic capital, among others. However, while these challenges are pervasive and well-entrenched across sub-Saharan Africa, one thing is certain from the overall findings in this book – *African journalism in the 21st century cannot be conceived of as anything but interactive, engaging and deliberately structured* (through 'generic technological affordances' and 'automated participatory practices') to enable audiences to engage with news in previously unseen ways. Thus, 'Whatever the yardstick one uses – a strict definition that says journalism must involve original reporting and an editorial filter, or a broader one that considers' audience's online comments on stories, microblogging, or even the banal affective activities of 'liking' and 'sharing' stories etc. – '*it's certain that audience participation in the news equation is on the upswing*' (Lasica 2003a, emphasis added).

There is no denying that in Africa, as elsewhere, journalism's purpose can no longer be simply about *informing* the public, in the traditional top-down fashion (Ryfe 2019), nor can journalists purport to be the sole arbiters of news. Likewise, audiences approach news online not just to read the main story but also with the fervent expectation to 'leave their own mark or trace' thanks to the multiple interactive options available to them (see Usher 2016). In this sense, *participatory journalism* can be seen as sustaining 'the idea that citizens [now] have a right to [*contribute* to] a news narrative' in ways that also challenge and decentre 'dominant news discourses' (Wall 2017, 137, emphasis added). The failure to embrace these changes by media organisations is akin to 'courting obscurity and potential irrelevance' (Peters 2011, 155). As Barney et al. argue, in a much broader sense, '*participation* has become a measure of the quality of our social situations and interactions, and has come to stand in for virtues that, under other conditions, might have names like equality, justice, fairness, community, or freedom' (2016, ix, emphasis added). In the context of news production and consumption, 'a lack of participation seems suspicious, strange, and disappointing – an impoverishment of democratic forms of citizenship' (p. ix). Equally, for journalists, there is an unwritten expectation to want to directly engage with readers or at least to monitor how they engage with one's stories. As we have shown in this book, this is also shaping and influencing the generation of news stories.

In some contexts, however, developments in AI are increasingly challenging and complicating the notion of user *participation* by exerting pressure on the agency of users – both journalists and audiences – hence calls for the close examining of algorithms and the development of ethical chatbots. All this entails 'new ways of thinking [about] and doing journalism' (Usher 2016, 5), with implications for news values and editorial decision making, albeit in ways that are not necessarily always obvious to the 'ordinary eye'. Indeed, the participatory practices and emerging forms of audience engagement have become 'the new normative' for African journalism in the 21st century. We are witnessing monumental shifts in the ontological foundations of journalism and the emergence of a 'new' form of journalism – a journalism foretold by American technology columnist and writer Dan Gillmor at the turn of the century, as *'tomorrow's journalism* [in which] professionals and gifted amateurs [operate] as partners' (cited in Lasica 2003b, emphasis added). A rare moment in contemporary history, where, as seen in Chapters 2 and 3, journalism's hegemony 'as gatekeeper of the news is threatened by not just new technology […] but, potentially, by the audience it serves' (Lasica 2003b). To use Gillmor's words,

> *[j]ournalism from the edges is taking us to a new place. The only thing certain is that we'll never return to the days when people are treated as passive vessels for content delivered by big media through one-way pipes – no matter how disruptive these changes may be for traditional media.*
>
> (cited in Lasica 2003b, emphasis added)

As we have seen throughout the book, these changes are not without radical normative and ethical dilemmas for news organisations and their journalists.

We should end by highlighting two key points that should echo at the back of one's mind while reflecting on the issues explored in this book. *First*, sub-Saharan Africa is a very complex region. This book thus carries with it the unavoidable risk of missing out on a number of important experiences across the region – it is simply impossible for a single book to capture the numerous experiences of *participatory journalism* across such a vast and complex area. *Second*, and even more importantly, the ephemeral and transient nature of digital technologies render it possible that some of the findings in the book will be overtaken by events even before it goes to press. That is a possibility we cannot escape in this era of rapid developments in digital technologies. Be that as it may, we hope that the book captures some of the salient contours of the emerging cultures and practices of *participatory journalism in Africa*, which, if nothing else, can serve as key reference points for further and ongoing explorations of related issues as the digital revolution unfolds.

References

Accone, Tanya (2000) 'Digital Dividends for Journalism in Africa'. *Nieman Reports*, 54 (4): 67–69.

Aitamurto, Tanja (2016) 'Crowdsourcing in Open Journalism: Benefits, Challenges and Value Creation'. In *The Routledge Companion to Digital Journalism Studies*, edited by Franklin, Bob and EldridgeII, Scott A., 185–193. London: Routledge.

Alhabash, Saleem and McAlister, Anna R. (2015) 'Redefining Virality in Less Broad Strokes: Predicting Viral Behavioural Intentions from Motivations and Uses of Facebook and Twitter'. *New Media & Society*, 17 (8): 1317–1339.

Allan, Stuart (2014) 'Foreword'. In *Online Journalism in Africa: Trends, Practices and Emerging Cultures*, edited by Mabweazara, Hayes M., Mudhai, Okoth F. and Whittaker, Jason, ix–x. London: Routledge.

Barney, Darin, Coleman, Gabriella, Ross, Christine, Sterne, Jonathan, and Tembeck, Tamar (2016) 'The Participatory Condition: An Introduction'. In *The Participatory Condition in the Digital Age*, edited by Barney, Darin, Coleman, Gabriella, Ross, Christine, Sterne, Jonathan and Tembeck, Tamar, vii–xxxix. Minneapolis: University of Minnesota Press.

Batsell, Jake (2015) *Engaged Journalism: Connecting with Digitally Empowered News Audiences*. New York: Columbia University Press.

Beaujon, Andrew (2019) 'The Washington Post's New Social Media Policy Forbids Disparaging Advertisers'. *Washingtonian*. Retrieved from: www.washingtonian.com/2017/06/27/the-washington-post-social-media-policy/ [accessed 17 May 2019].

Beckett, Charlie (2008) *Supermedia: Saving Journalism So It Can Save the World*. Oxford: Blackwell Publishing.

Berger, Guy (2005) 'Powering African Newsrooms: Theorising How Southern African Journalists make use of ICTs for Newsgathering'. In *Doing Digital Journalism: How Southern African Newsgatherers are using ICTs*, edited by Guy Berger, 1–14. Grahamstown: High Way Africa.

Besaw, Clayton and Filitz, John (2019) 'AI & Global Governance: AI in Africa is a Double-Edged Sword'. United Nations University, Centre for Policy

Research. Retrieved from https://cpr.unu.edu/ai-in-africa-is-a-double-edged-sword.html [accessed 20 July 2020].

Bijker, Wiebe E. (1995) *Of Bicycles, Bakelite and Bulbs: Towards a Theory of Sociotechnical Change.* Cambridge: MIT Press.

Bivens, Rena K (2008) 'The Internet, Mobile Phones and Blogging'. *Journalism Practice*, 2 (1): 113–129.

Blanchett Neheli, Nicole (2018) 'News by Numbers'. *Digital Journalism*, 6 (8): 1041–1051.

boyd, danah (2009) 'Social Media is Here to Stay... Now What?' Microsoft Research Tech Fest, Redmond, Washington, February 26. www.danah. org/papers/talks/MSRTechFest2009.html [accessed 27 April 2020]

Brabham, Daren C. (2012) 'Motivations for Participation in a Crowdsourcing Application to Improve Public Engagement in Transit Planning'. *Journal of Applied Communication Research*, 40 (3): 307–328.

Bradshaw, Samantha and Howard, Phillip (2018) 'The Global Organization of Social Media Disinformation Campaigns'. *Journal of International Affairs*, 71 (1): 23–32.

Brinkman, Inge, Lamoureaux, Daniela M. and de Bruijn, Mirjam (2011) 'Local Stories, Global Discussion: Websites, Politics and Identity in African Contexts'. In *Popular Media, Democracy and Development in Africa*, edited by Wasserman, Herman, 236–252. London: Routledge.

Broersma, Marcel and EldridgeII, Scott (2019) 'Journalism and Social Media: Redistribution of Power?' *Media and Communication*, 7 (1): 193–197.

Broussard, Meredith, Diakopoulos, Nicholas, Guzman, Andrea L., Abebe, Rediet, Dupagne, Michel and Chuan, Ching-Hua (2019) 'Artificial Intelligence and Journalism'. *Journalism and Mass Communication Quarterly*, 96 (3): 673–695.

Bruns, Axel (2008) 'The Active Audience: Transforming Journalism from Gatekeeping to Gatewatching'. In *Making Online News: The Ethnography of New Media Production*, edited by Paterson, Chris and Domingo, David, 171–197. New York: Peter Lang.

Bruns, Axel and Highfield, Timothy (2012) 'Blogs, Twitter, and Breaking News: The Produsage of Citizen Journalism'. In *Producing Theory in a Digital World: The Intersection of Audiences and Production in Contemporary Theory*, edited by Lind, R. A., 15–32. New York: Peter Lang Publishing.

Bruns, Axel and Nuernbergk, Christian (2019) 'Political Journalists and Their Social Media Audiences: New Power Relations?' *Media and Communication*, 7 (1): 198–212.

Bucher, Taina (2017) 'The Algorithmic Imaginary: Exploring the Ordinary Affects of Facebook Algorithms'. *Information, Communication & Society*, 20 (1): 30–44.

Cambridge Consultants (2019) *Use of AI in online Content Moderation: 2019 Report Produced on Behalf of OFCom.* Retrieved from: www.ofcom.org.uk/__data/assets/pdf_file/0028/157249/cambridge-consultants-ai-content-moderation.pdf [accessed on 18 May 2020].

Cammaerts, Bart (2008) 'Critiques on the Participatory Potentials of Web 2.0'. *Communication, Culture & Critique*, 1 (4): 358–377.

Campbell, Vincent (2004) *Information Age Journalism: Journalism in an International Context.* London: Arnold.

Canter, Lily (2013) 'The Misconception of Online Comment Threads: Content and Control on Local Newspaper Websites', *Journalism Practice*, 7 (5): 604–619.

Carlson, Matt (2018) 'Confronting Measurable Journalism'. *Digital Journalism*, 6 (4): 406–417.

Carpentier, Nico (2011) *Media and Participation: A Site of Ideological Democratic Struggle.* Bristol: Intellect.

Carpentier, Nico, Melo, Ana Duarte and Ribeiro, Fabio (2019) 'Rescuing Participation: A Critique on the Dark Participation Concept'. *Comunicação e Sociedade*, 36: 17–35.

Chadwick, Paul (2018) 'As Technology Develops, So Must Journalists' Codes of Ethics'. *The Guardian.* Retrieved from: www.theguardian.com/commentis free/2018/jan/21/technology-codes-ethics-ai-artificial-intelligence [accessed 20 June 2020].

Chari, Tendai (2009) 'Ethical Challenges Facing Zimbabwean Media in the Context of the Internet'. *Global Media Journal: African Edition*, 3 (1): 1–34.

Chesney, Robert and Citron, Danielle K (2018). 'Disinformation on Steroids: The Threat of Deep Fakes, Cyber Brief'. Council on Foreign Relations. Retrieved from: www.cfr.org/report/deep-fake-disinformation-steroids [accessed 20 June 2020].

Clerwall, Christer (2014) 'Enter the Robot Journalist'. *Journalism Practice*, 8 (5): 519–531.

Cohen, Sarah, Hamilton, James T. and Turner, Fred (2011) 'Computational Journalism'. *Communications of the ACM*, 54 (10): 66–71.

Conboy, Martin (2013) *Journalism Studies: The Basics.* London: Routledge.

Cornwall, Andreas (2002) 'Making Spaces, Changing Places: Situating Participation in Development', IDS Working Paper 173. Brighton: Institute of Development Studies.

Curran, James (2016) *The Internet of Dreams: Reinterpreting the Internet, in Misunderstanding the Internet*, edited by Curran, James, Fenton, Natalie and Freedman, Des, 1–47. London: Routledge.

Denisova, Anastasia (2020) 'How to Define 'Viral' for Media Studies?' *Westminster Papers in Communication and Culture*, 15 (1): 1–4.

Deuze, Mark (2003) 'The Web and its Journalisms: Considering the Consequences of Different Types of Newsmedia Online'. *New Media & Society*, 5 (2): 203–230.

Deuze, Mark and Dimoudi, Christina (2002) 'Online Journalists in the Netherlands: Towards a Profile of a New Profession'. *Journalism: Theory, Practice & Criticism*, 3 (1): 85–100.

Domingo, David (2008) 'Inventing Online Journalism: A Constructivist Approach to the Development of Online News'. In *Making Online News:*

The Ethnography of New Media Production, edited by Paterson, Chris and Domingo, David, 15–28. New York: Peter Lang.

Dörr, Konstantin N. (2016) 'Mapping the Field of Algorithmic Journalism'. *Digital Journalism*, 4 (6): 700–722.

Drabinski, Emily (2018) 'Ideologies of Boring Things: The Internet and Infrastructures of Race'. *Los Angeles Review of Books*, https://lareviewofbooks. org/article/ideologies-of-boring-things-the-internet-and-infrastructures-of-race/ [accessed 14 February 2020].

Duff, Alistair S. (2008) 'The Normative Crisis of the Information Society', *Cyberpsychology: Journal of Psychosocial Research on Cyberspace*, 2 (1). Retrieved from: http://cyberpsychology.eu/view.php?cisloclanku =2008051201 & article=1 [accessed 10 December 2016].

Eko, Lyombe (2010) 'The Art of Criticism: How African Cartoons Discursively Constructed African Media Realities in the Post-Cold War Era'. *Critical African Studies*, 2 (4): 65–91.

Ellis, Stephen (1989) 'Tuning in to Pavement Radio'. *African Affairs*, 88 (352): 321–330.

Fairrington, Brian (2009) *Drawing Cartoons and Comics for Dummies*. Hoboken: Wiley Publishing.

Farwell, Beatrice (1989) *The Charged Image: French lithographic Caricature*. Santa Barbara: Santa Barbara Museum of Art.

Fenton, Natalie (2010) 'Drowning of Waving? New Media, Journalism and Democracy'. In *New Media, Old News: Journalism & Democracy in the Digital Age*, edited by Fenton, Natalie, 3–16. London: Sage.

Fiegerman, Seth (2014) *No Comment: Why News Websites are Ditching Comment Sections*. Retrieved from: https://mashable.com/2014/12/17/no-comm ent/ [accessed 21 November 2019].

Ford, Heather and Hutchinson, Jonathon (2019) 'Newsbots That Mediate Journalist and Audience Relationships'. *Digital Journalism*, 7 (8): 1013–1031.

Fraser, Nancy (1990) 'Rethinking the Public Sphere: A Contribution to the Critique of Actually Existing Democracy'. *Social Text*, 25/26: 56–80.

Frere, Marie Soleil (2014) 'Online Forums: How the Voices of Readers are Reshaping the Sphere of Public Debate in Burkina Faso'. In *Online Journalism in Africa: Trends, Practices and Emerging Cultures*, edited by Mabweazara, Hayes M., Mudhai, Okoth F. and Whittaker, Jason, 237–258. London: Routledge.

Fuchs, Christians (2017) *Social Media: A Critical Introduction*. London: Sage.

Gaventa, John (2006) 'Perspectives on Participation and Citizenship'. In *Participatory Citizenship: Identity, Exclusion, Inclusion*, edited in Mohanty, Ranjita and Tandon, Rajesh. 51–67. London: Sage.

Gilfillan, Colum S. (1935) *The Sociology of Invention*. Chicago: Follett Publishing Company.

Goode, Luke (2009) 'Social News, Citizen Journalism and Democracy', *New Media & Society*, 11 (8): 1287–1305.

Gulyas, Agnes (2013) 'The Influence of Professional Variables on Journalists' Uses and Views of Social Media'. *Digital Journalism*, 1 (2): 270–285.

Habermas, Jurgen (1989) *The Structural Transformation of the Public Sphere: An Inquiry into a Category of Bourgeois Society* (trans. by Burger, T. with the Assistance of Lawrence, F.). Cambridge: Polity Press.

Hall, Stuart, Critcher, Chas, Jefferson, Tony, Clarke, John N. and Roberts, Brian (1978) *Policing the Crisis: Mugging, the State, and Law and Order.* London: Routledge and Kegan Paul.

Hammett, Daniel (2010) 'Political Cartoons, Post-Colonialism and Critical African Studies'. *Critical African Studies*, 2 (4): 1–26.

Harcup, Tony (2008) 'Reporters Need to Ask What They're Not Being Told'. *Press Gazette*, 18 February. Retrieved from: www.pressgazette.co.uk/story. asp?sectioncode=1&storycode=40268 [accessed 10 July 2017].

He, Baogang (2006) 'Participatory and Deliberative Institutions in China'. In *The Search for Deliberation Democracy in China*, edited by Leib, Ethan J. and He, Baogang, 175–196. New York: Palgrave MacMillan.

Hermida, Alfred (2010) 'Twittering the News: The Emergence of Ambient Journalism'. *Journalism Practice*, 4 (3): 297–308.

Hermida, Alfred (2011a) 'Mechanisms of Participation: How Audience Options Shape the Coversation'. In *Participatory Journalism: Guarding Open Gates at Online Newspapers*, edited by Singer, Jane, *et al.*, 13–33. New York: Wiley-Blackwell.

Hermida, Alfred (2011b) 'Fluid Spaces, Fluid Journalism: The Role of the "Active Recipient" in Participatory Journalism'. In *Participatory Journalism: Guarding Open Gates at Online Newspapers*, edited by Singer, Jane, *et al.*, 177–191. New York: Wiley-Blackwell.

Hermida, Alfred, and Thurman, Neil (2008) 'A Clash of Cultures: The Integration of User-Generated Content Within Professional Journalistic Frameworks at British Newspaper Websites'. *Journalism Practice*, 2 (3): 343–356.

Hille, Sanne and Bakker, Piet (2014) 'Engaging the Social News User'. *Journalism Practice*, 8 (5): 563–572.

Ibelema, Minabere (2008) *The African Press, Civic Cynicism, and Democracy.* New York: Palgrave Macmillan.

Jenkins, Henry (2006) *Convergence Culture: Where Old and New Media Collide.* New York: New York University Press.

Jones, Bronwyn and Jones, Rhianne (2019) 'Public Service Chatbots: Automating Conversation with BBC News'. *Digital Journalism*, 7 (8): 1032–1053.

Jönsson, Anna Maria and Örnebring, Henrik (2011) 'User-Generated Content and the News: Empowerment of Citizens or an Interactive Illusion?' *Journalism Practice*, 5 (2): 127–144.

Kammer, Aske (2013) 'Audience Participation in the Production of Online News Towards a Typology'. *Nordicom Review*, 34: 113–126.

Kasoma, Francis P. (1996) 'The Foundations of African Ethics (Afriethics) and the Professional Practice of Journalism: The Case of Society-Centred Media Morality'. *Africa Media Review*, 10 (3): 93–116.

Kawamoto, Kevin (2003) *Digital Journalism: Emerging Media and the Changing Horizons of Journalism.* Lanham: Rowman & Littlefield.

Keller, Tobias R. and Klinger, Ulrike (2019) 'Social Bots in Election Campaigns: Theoretical, Empirical, and Methodological Implications'. *Political Communication*, 36 (1): 171–189.

Ksiazek, Thomas B. and Springer, Nina (2020) *User Comments and Moderation in Digital Journalism: Disruptive Engagement*. London: Routledge.

Kwet, Michael (2019) 'Digital Colonialism: US Empire and the New Imperialism in the Global South'. *Race & Class*, 60 (4): 3–26.

Lackaff, Derek (2005) 'Norm Maintenance in Online Communities: A Review of Moderation Regimes'. Research Paper. Melbourne: La Trobe University.

Lasica, Joseph D. (2003a) 'What is Participatory Journalism?' *Online Journalism Review*. Retrieved from: www.ojr.org/ojr/workplace/1060217106.php [accessed 20 October 2019].

Lasica, Joseph D. (2003b) 'Participatory Journalism Puts the Reader in the Driver's Seat', *Online Journalism Review*. Retrieved from: www.ojr.org/ojr/workplace/1060218311.php [accessed 10 July 2019].

Lewis, Seth C. (2012) 'The Tension Between Professional Control and Open Participation: Jornalism and its Boundaries'. *Information, Communication & Society*, 15 (6): 836–866.

Lewis, Seth C. (2015) 'Journalism in an Era of Big Data: Cases, Concepts, and Critiques'. *Digital Journalism*, 3 (3): 321–330.

Lokot, Tetyana and Diakopoulos, Nicholas (2016) 'News Bots'. *Digital Journalism*, 4 (6): 682–699.

Mabweazara, Hayes M. (2011) 'The Internet in the Print Newsroom: Trends, Practices and Emerging Cultures in Zimbabwe'. In *Making Online News: Newsroom Ethnography in the Second Decade of Internet Journalism*, edited by Domingo, David and Paterson, Chris, 57–469. New York: Peter Lang.

Mabweazara, Hayes M. (2013) 'Normative Dilemmas and Issues for Zimbabwean Print Journalism in the "Information Society" Era'. *Digital Journalism*, 1 (1): 135–151.

Mabweazara, Hayes M. (2014) 'Zimbabwe's Mainstream Press in the "Social Media Age": Emerging Practices and Cultures'. In *Online Journalism in Africa: Trends, Practices and Emerging Cultures*, edited by Mabweazara, Hayes M., Mudhai, Okoth F. and Whittaker, Jason, 65–86. London: Routledge.

Mabweazara, Hayes M. (2015a) 'African Journalism in the "Digital Era": Charting a Research Agenda'. *African Journalism Studies*, 36 (1): 11–17.

Mabweazara, Hayes M. (2015b) 'Charting Theoretical Directions for Examining African Journalism in the "Digital Era"'. *Journalism Practice*, 9 (1): 106–122.

Mabweazara, Hayes M. (2017) 'Context, Prospects and Contradictions: Histories of Internet-Based Digital Journalism Research in Africa', in *The Routledge Companion to Global Internet Histories*, edited by Gerard, Goggin and McLelland, Mark, 399–411. London: Routledge.

Mabweazara, Hayes M. (2018) 'Reinvigorating "Age-Old Questions": African Journalism Cultures and the Fallacy of Global Normative Homogeneity'. In

Newsmaking Cultures in Africa: Normative Trends in the Dynamics of Socio-Political & Economic Struggles, edited by Mabweazara, Hayes M., 1–27. London: Palgrave Macmillan.

Mabweazara, Hayes M., Mudhai, Okoth F. and Whittaker, Jason (eds.) (2014) *Online Journalism in Africa: Trends, Practices and Emerging Cultures.* London: Routledge.

MacKenzie, Donald and Wajcman, Judy (eds.) (1999) *The Social Shaping of Technology.* Buckingham: Open University Press.

Mambwe, Elastus (2019) 'Investigating the Use and Impact of Social Media in Zambian Newsrooms Between 2011–2013'. *International Journal of Multidisciplinary Research and Development*, 6 (4): 30–37.

Mandiberg, Michael (ed.) (2012) *The Social Media Reader.* New York: New York University Press.

Mano, Winston (2007) 'Popular Music as Journalism in Zimbabwe'. *Journalism Studies*, 8 (1): 61–78.

Mare, Admire (2014) 'New Media Technologies and Internal Newsroom Creativity in Mozambique', *Digital Journalism*, 2 (1): 12–28.

Mare, Admire (2016) *Facebook, Youth and Political Action: A Comparative Study of Zimbabwe and South Africa.* PhD dissertation, Rhodes University, Grahamstown, South Africa.

Mare, Admire (2020) 'Popular Communication in Africa: An Empirical and Theoretical Exposition'. *Annals of the International Communication Association*, 44 (1): 81–99.

Mare, Admire and Matsilele, Trust (2020) 'Digital Media and the July 2018 Elections in 'Post-Mugabe' Zimbabwe'. In *Social Media and Elections in Africa: Theoretical and Methodological Perspectives* (Volume 1), edited by Ndlela, M. N. and Mano, Winston. London: Palgrave MacMillan.

Mare, Admire, Mabweazara, Hayes M. and Moyo, Dumisani (2019) '"Fake News" and Cyber-Propaganda in Sub-Saharan Africa: Recentering the Research Agenda'. *African Journalism Studies*, 41 (4): 1–12.

Markham, Tim (2017) *Media and Everyday Life.* London: Palgrave.

Maweu, Jacinta Mwende (2019) '"Fake Elections"? Cyber Propaganda, Disinformation and the 2017 General Elections in Kenya'. *African Journalism Studies*, 40 (4): 62–76.

McElroy, Kathleen (2013) 'Where Old (Gatekeepers) Meets New (Media): Herding Reader Comments into Print'. *Journalism Practice*, 7 (6): 755–771.

McKenna, Brad, Myers, Michael D. and Newman, Michael (2017) 'Social Media in Qualitative Research: Challenges and Recommendations'. *Information and Organisation*, 27 (2): 87–99.

McLellan, Michele and Porter, Tim (2007) *News, Improved: How America's Newsrooms Are Learning to Change.* Washington: CQ Press.

Meikle, Graham (2016) *Social Media: Communication, Sharing and Visibility.* London: Routledge.

Meikle, Graham and Young, Sherman (2012) *Media Convergence: Networked Digital Media in Everyday Life.* New York: Palgrave Macmillan.

Milioni, Dimitra L., Vadratsikas, Konstantinos and Papa, Venetia (2012) "'Their Two Cents Worth": Exploring User Agency in Readers' Comments in Online News Media'. *Observatorio*, 6 (3): 21–47.

Moyo, Dumisani (2009) 'Citizen Journalism and the Parallel Market of Information in Zimbabwe's 2008 Election'. *Journalism Studies*, 10 (4): 551–567.

Moyo, Dumisani, Mare, Admire and Matsilele, Trust (2019) 'Analytics-Driven Journalism? Editorial Metrics and the Reconfiguration of Online News Production Practices in African Newsrooms', *Digital Journalism*, 7 (4): 490–506.

Moyo, Last (2020) 'The End of the Public Sphere: Social Media, Civic Virtue, and the Democratic Divide'. In *Digital Inequalities in the Global South, Global Transformations in Media and Communication Research – A Palgrave and IAMCR Series*, edited by Ragnedda, Massimo and Gladkova, Anna, 269–288. Cham: Palgrave Macmillan.

Mudhai, Okoth F. (2011) 'Immediacy and Openness in a Digital Africa: Networked Convergent Journalisms in Kenya'. *Journalism: Theory, Practice and Criticism*, 12 (6): 674–691.

Mudhai, Okoth F. (2014). 'Immediacy and Openness in a Digital Africa: Networked-Convergent Journalisms in Kenya'. In *Online Journalism in Africa: Trends, Practices and Emerging Cultures*, edited by Mabweazara, Hayes M., Mudhai, Okoth F. and Whittaker, Jason, 123–140. London: Routledge.

Mudhai, Okoth F. and Nyabuga, George (2001) 'The Internet: Triumphs and Trials for Journalism in Kenya'. Paper Presented at the Annual Highway Africa Conference, Rhodes University. Retrieved from: www.highwayafrica. org.za/presentations/55.doc [accessed 20 June 2015].

Ncube, Lyton (2019) 'Digital Media, Fake News and Pro-Movement for Democratic Change (MDC) Alliance Cyber-Propaganda during the 2018 Zimbabwe Election'. *African Journalism Studies*, 40 (4): 44–61.

Ndlela, Martin N. (2020) 'Social Media Algorithms, Bots and Elections in Africa'. In *Social Media and Elections* (Volume 1), edited by Ndlela, Martin, N. and Mano, Winston. London: Palgrave MacMillan.

Ngwira, Emmanuel and Lipenga, KenJr (2018) 'A Country Laughing at Itself: Malawian Humour in the Digital Age'. *English Studies in Africa*, 61 (2): 21–35.

Noble, Safiya U. (2018) *Algorithms of Oppression: How Search Engines Reinforce Racism*. New York: New York University Press.

Nomai, Afsheen Joseph (2008) *Culture Jamming: Ideological Struggle and the Possibilities for Social Change*. Austin: University of Texas.

Nyamnjoh, Francis B. (1999) 'African Cultural Studies, Cultural Studies in Africa: How to Make a Useful Difference'. *Critical Arts: A Journal of Cultural Studies in Africa*, 13 (1): 15–39.

Nyamnjoh, Francis B. (2005) *Africa's Media: Democracy and the Politics of Belonging*. London: Zed Books.

Obonyo, Levi (2011) 'Towards a Theory of Communication for Africa: The Challenges for Emerging Democracies', *Communicatio*, 37 (1): 1–20.

Oeldorf-Hirsch, Anne (2018) 'The Role of Engagement in Learning from Active and Incidental News Exposure on Social Media'. *Mass Communication and Society*, 21 (2): 225–247.

Olsson, Tobias and Svensson, Anders (2012) 'Producing Prod-Users: Conditional Participation in a Web 2.0 Consumer Community'. *Javnost – The Public: Journal of the European Institute for Communication and Culture*, 19 (3): 41–58.

O'Reilly, Tim (2005) *What is Web 2.0?* Retrieved from: http://oreilly.com/web2/archive/what-is-web-20.html [accessed 14 February 2020].

Orlikowski, Wanda J. (1992) 'The Duality of Technology: Rethinking the Concept of Technology in Organizations'. *Organization Science*, 3 (3): 398–427.

Parks, Lisa and Mukherjee, Rahul (2017) 'From Platform Jumping to Self-Censorship: Internet Freedom, Social Media, and Circumvention Practices in Zambia'. *Communication and Critical/Cultural Studies*, 14 (3): 221–237.

Paterson, Chris (2008) 'Introduction: Why Ethnography?' In *Making Online News: The Ethnography of New Media Production*, edited by Paterson, Chris and Domingo, David, 1–11. New York: Peter Lang.

Paterson, Chris (2013) 'Journalism and Social Media in the African Context'. *Ecquid Novi: African Journalism Studies*, 34 (1): 1–6.

Pavlik, John V. (2000) 'The Impact of Technology on Journalism'. *Journalism Studies*, 1 (2): 229–237.

Peters, Justin (2011) 'On Facebook and Freedom: Why Journalists Should Not Surrender to the Walmarts of the Web', *Columbia Journalism Review*, 50 (4): 155–160.

Pinch, Trevor L. and Bijker, Weibe E. (1984) 'The Social Construction of Facts and Artifacts: Or How Sociology of Science and the Sociology of Technology Might Benefit Each Other?' *Social Studies of Science*, 14: 399–441.

Postema, Stijn and Deuze, Mark (2020) 'Artistic Journalism: Confluence in Forms, Values and Practices', *Journalism Studies*, 21 (10): 1305–1322.

Quandt, Thorsten (2018) 'Dark Participation'. *Media and Communication*, 6 (4): 36–48.

Reich, Zvi (2011) 'User Comments: The Transformation of Participatory Space'. In *Participatory Journalism: Guarding Open Gates at Online Newspapers*, edited by Singer, Jane B., *et al.*, 96–117. Malden: Wiley-Blackwell.

Renner, Nausicaa (2017) 'As AI Enters Newsrooms, Journalists Have Urgent Responsibility'. Columbia Journalism Review. Retrieved from www.cjr.org/tow_center/artificial-intelligence-newsrooms.php [accessed 7 July 2020].

Reporters Without Borders (2016) *Authorities Hound Independent Journalists at Home and Abroad*. Retrieved from: https://rsf.org/en/news/authorities-hound-independent-journalists-home-and-abroad [accessed 21 July 2020].

Robinson, Sue (2011) 'Convergence Crises: News Work and News Space in the Digitally Transforming Newsroom'. *Journal of Communication*, 61 (6): 1122–1141.

Ronderos, Maria Teresa (2019) 'How Innovative Newsrooms Are Using Artificial Intelligence'. Investigative Journalism Network. Retrieved from https: //gijn. org/2019/01/22/artificial-intelligence-demands-genuine-journalism/# [accessed 7 July 2020].

Rosen, Jay (2006) 'The People Formerly Known as the Audience'. *PressThink.* http://journalism.nyu.edu/pubzone/weblogs/pressthink/2006/06/27/ppl_frmr. html [accessed 8 September 2019].

Ryfe, David (2019) 'The Ontology of Journalism'. *Journalism: Theory, Practice & Criticism*, 20 (1): 206–209.

Santana, Arthur D. (2011) 'Online Readers' Comments Represent New Opinion Pipeline'. *Newspaper Research Journal*, 32 (3): 66–81.

Schudson, Michael (2000) 'The Sociology of News Production Revisited (Again)'. In *Mass Media and Society*, edited by Curran, James and Gurevitch, Michael, 175–200. London: Arnold.

Schwab, Klaus (2015) *The Fourth Industrial Revolution.* New York: Foreign Affairs.

Sherwood, Merryn and Nicholson, Matthew (2012) 'Web 2.0 Platforms and the Work of Newspaper Sport Journalists'. *Journalism: Theory, Practice & Criticism*, 14 (7): 942–959.

Shi, Zhan, Rui, Huaxia, and Whinston, Andrew B. (2014) 'Content Sharing in a Social Broadcasting Environment: Evidence From Twitter'. *MIS Quarterly*, 38 (1): 123–142.

Sigal, Leon V. (1973) *Reporters and Officials: The Organisation and Politics of News.* London: D.C. Heath and Company.

Singer, Jane B. (1997) 'Still Guarding the Gate? The Newspaper Journalist's Role in an On-line World'. *Convergence*, 3 (1): 72–89.

Singer, Jane B. (2009) 'Separate Spaces: Discourse About the 2007 Scottish Elections on a National Newspaper Website'. *International Journal of Press/ Politics*, 14 (4): 477–496.

Singer, Jane B. *et al.* (2011) 'Introduction: Sharing the Road'. In *Participatory Journalism: Guarding Open Gates at Online Newspapers*, edited by Singer, Jane, *et al.*, 1–9. New York: Wiley-Blackwell.

Srinivasan, Sharath and Diepeveen, Stephanie (2018) 'The Power of the "Audience-Public": Interactive Radio in Africa'. *The International Journal of Press/Politics*, 23 (3): 389–412.

Suau, Jaume and Pere, Masip (2014) 'Exploring Participatory Journalism in Mediterranean Countries'. *Journalism Practice*, 8 (6): 670–687.

Sullivan, Margaret (2012) 'After an Outburst on Twitter, The Times Reinforces Its Social Media Guidelines'. *The New York Times.* Retrieved from: https://publi ceditor.blogs.nytimes.com/2012/10/17/after-an-outburst-on-twitter-the-times-re inforces-its-social-media-guidelines/ [accessed 20 April 2020].

Thompson, John B. (2020) 'Mediated Interaction in the Digital Age'. *Theory, Culture & Society*, 37 (1): 3–28.

Thurman, Neil, Cornia, Alessio and Kunert, Jessica (2016) *Journalists in the UK.* Oxford: Reuters.

Usher, Nikki (2016) *Interactive Journalism: Hackers, Data, and Code*. Urbana: University of Illinois Press.

van Dijck, Jose (2013) *The Culture of Connectivity: A Critical History of Social Media*. Oxford: Oxford University Press.

van Dijk, Jan G. M. (2006) 'Digital Divide Research, Achievements and Shortcomings'. *Poetics*, 34 (4–5): 221–235.

Verclas, Katrin and Mechael, Patricia (2008) 'A Mobile Voice: The Use of Mobile Phones in Citizen Media'. Washington: United States Agency for International Development. Retrieved from: www.usaid.gov/about_usaid/hrd/A_Mobile_ Voice.pdf. [accessed 20 May 2010].

Wall, Melissa (2017) 'Mapping Citizen and Participatory Journalism in Newsrooms, Classrooms and Beyond'. *Journalism Practice*, 11 (2–3): 134–141.

WAN-IFRA (World Association of Newspapers and News Publishers) (2019) 'Trends in Newsrooms #2: AI in the Newsroom'. World Editors Forum. Retrieved from: www.wan-ifra.org/reports/2019/09/30/trends-in-newsrooms-2-ai-in-the-newsroom [accessed 25 November 2018].

Wasserman, Herman (2011) 'Mobile Phones, Popular Media, and Everyday African Democracy: Transmissions and Transgressions'. *Popular Communication*, 9 (2): 146–158.

Wasserman, Herman (2018) *Media, Geopolitics, and Power: A View from the Global South*. Urbana, Chicago: University of Illinois Press.

Wasserman, Herman (2020) 'Laughter in the Time of a Pandemic: Why South Africans are Joking About Coronavirus'. *The Conversation*. Retrieved from: https://theconversation.com/laughter-in-the-time-of-a-pandemic-why-south-africans-are-joking-about-coronavirus-133528 [accessed 20 June 2020]

Westlund, Oscar and Ekström, Mats (2018) 'News and Participation through and beyond Proprietary Platforms in an Age of Social Media'. *Media and Communication*, 6 (4): 1–10.

Westlund, Oscar and Murschetz, Paul C. (2019) 'Reviewing the Nexus of Participatory Journalism and Mediatized Engagement'. *JOCIS – Journal of Creative Industries and Cultural Studies*, 4: 54–73.

Willems, Wendy (2011) 'Political Jokes in Zimbabwe'. In *Encyclopaedia of Social Movement Media*, edited by Downing, John D.H., 410–412. Los Angeles: Sage.

Willems, Wendy (2013) 'Participation – in What? Radio, Convergence and the Corporate Logic of Audience Input through New Media in Zambia'. *Telematics and Informatics*, 30 (3): 223–231.

Willems, Wendy and Mano, Winston (2016) 'Decolonizing and Provincializing Audience and Internet Studies: Contextual Approaches from African Vantage'. In *Everyday Media Culture in Africa: Audiences and Users*, edited by Willems, Wendy and Mano, Winston, 1–26. London: Routledge.

Young, Mary L. and Hermida, Alfred (2014) 'From Mr. and Mrs. Outlier to Central Tendencies. Computational Journalism and Crime Reporting at the Los Angeles Times'. *Digital Journalism*, 3 (3): 381–397.

Zamith, Rodrigo (2018) 'Quantified Audiences in News Production: A Synthesis and Research Agenda'. *Digital Journalism*, 6 (4): 418–435.

Zelizer, Barbie (2017) *What Journalism Could Be*. Cambridge: Polity.

Zuboff, Shoshana (2019) *The Age of Surveillance Capitalism: The Fight for a Human Future at the New Frontier of Power*. New York: Public Affairs.

Index

For Product Safety Concerns and Information please contact our EU
representative GPSR@taylorandfrancis.com
Taylor & Francis Verlag GmbH, Kaufingerstraße 24, 80331 München, Germany

www.ingramcontent.com/pod-product-compliance
Ingram Content Group UK Ltd.
Pitfield, Milton Keynes, MK11 3LW, UK
UKHW021423080625
459435UK00011B/141